The Security Intelligence Handbook

Third Edition

How to Disrupt Adversaries and
Reduce Risk With Security Intelligence

Edited by Jeff May
Cover and Design by Lucas Clauser
Foreword by Christopher Ahlberg, Ph.D.

CYBEREDGE PRESS

The Security Intelligence Handbook, Third Edition

Published by:
CyberEdge Group, LLC
1997 Annapolis Exchange Parkway
Suite 300
Annapolis, MD 21401
(800) 327-8711
www.cyber-edge.com

Copyright © 2020, CyberEdge Group, LLC. All rights reserved. Definitive Guide™ and the CyberEdge Press logo are trademarks of CyberEdge Group, LLC in the United States and other countries. All other trademarks and registered trademarks are the property of their respective owners.

Except as permitted under the United States Copyright Act of 1976, no part of this publication may be reproduced, stored in a retrieval system or transmitted in any form or by any means, electronic, mechanical, photocopying, recording, scanning or otherwise, without the prior written permission of the publisher. Requests to the publisher for permission should be addressed to Permissions Department, CyberEdge Group, 1997 Annapolis Exchange Parkway, Suite 300, Annapolis, MD, 21401 or transmitted via email to info@cyber-edge.com.

LIMIT OF LIABILITY/DISCLAIMER OF WARRANTY: THE PUBLISHER AND THE AUTHOR MAKE NO REPRESENTATIONS OR WARRANTIES WITH RESPECT TO THE ACCURACY OR COMPLETENESS OF THE CONTENTS OF THIS WORK AND SPECIFICALLY DISCLAIM ALL WARRANTIES, INCLUDING WITHOUT LIMITATION WARRANTIES OF FITNESS FOR A PARTICULAR PURPOSE. THE ADVICE AND STRATEGIES CONTAINED HEREIN MAY NOT BE SUITABLE FOR EVERY SITUATION. NEITHER THE PUBLISHER NOR THE AUTHOR SHALL BE LIABLE FOR DAMAGES ARISING HEREFROM. THE FACT THAT AN ORGANIZATION OR WEBSITE IS REFERRED TO IN THIS WORK AS A CITATION AND/OR A POTENTIAL SOURCE OF FURTHER INFORMATION DOES NOT MEAN THAT THE AUTHOR OR THE PUBLISHER ENDORSES THE INFORMATION THE ORGANIZATION OR WEBSITE MAY PROVIDE OR RECOMMENDATIONS IT MAY MAKE. FURTHER, READERS SHOULD BE AWARE THAT INTERNET WEBSITES LISTED IN THIS WORK MAY HAVE CHANGED OR DISAPPEARED BETWEEN WHEN THIS WORK WAS WRITTEN AND WHEN IT IS READ.

For general information on CyberEdge Group research and marketing consulting services, or to create a custom *Definitive Guide* book for your organization, contact our sales department at 800-327-8711 or info@cyber-edge.com.

ISBN: 978-1-948939-15-7 (paperback)
ISBN: 978-1-948939-16-4 (eBook)

Printed in the United States of America.

10 9 8 7 6 5 4 3 2 1

Publisher's Acknowledgements

CyberEdge Group thanks the following individuals for their respective contributions:

Copy Editor: Susan Shuttleworth
Graphic Design: Debbi Stocco
Production Coordinator: Jon Friedman

Acknowledgements

This book's publication was made possible by the Recorded Future personnel who provided their insight and expertise to this third edition, as well as previous editions. They include: **Lucas Clauser** (designer), **Brendan Gibson** (contributor), **Levi Gundert** (contributor), **Allan Liska** (contributor), **Jeff May** (editor), **Maggie McDaniel** (contributor), **Zane Pokorny** (past editor and contributor), **John Wetzel** (contributor), and **Ellen Wilson** (contributor).

Foreword by **Dr. Christopher Ahlberg**, co-founder and CEO, Recorded Future.

Table of Contents

Acknowledgements	iii
Foreword to the Third Edition	viii
Introduction	xi

Section 1: What Is Security Intelligence?

Chapter 1: What Is Security Intelligence?	**3**
Visibility Into Threats Before They Strike	3
Actionable Facts and Insights	5
More than data or information	5
Security Intelligence: The Process	6
A collaborative process and framework	6
360-degree visibility	7
Extensive automation and integration	7
Alignment with the organization and security use cases	8
Who Benefits From Security Intelligence?	8
Chapter 2: Types and Sources	**11**
Two Types of Security Intelligence	11
Operational security intelligence	11
Strategic security intelligence	12
The Role of Threat Data Feeds	13
The Role of Private Channels and the Dark Web	15
Chapter 3: The Security Intelligence Lifecycle	**17**
The Six Phases of the Security Intelligence Lifecycle	17
Direction	18
Collection	19
Processing	21
Analysis	21
Dissemination	22
Feedback	23
Tools and People	23

Section 2: Applications of Security Intelligence

Chapter 4: SecOps Intelligence Part 1 – Triage	**27**
Responsibilities of the SecOps Team	28
The Overwhelming Volume of Alerts	29
Context Is King	30
Triage requires lots of context	30
Use case: Correlating and enriching alerts	31
Shortening the "Time to No"	33

Table of Contents | v

Chapter 5: SecOps Intelligence Part 2 – Response   35

Continuing Challenges   36
   The skills gap   36
   Rising response times   36
   A piecemeal approach   37
The Reactivity Problem   37
Minimizing Reactivity in Incident Response   38
   Identification of probable threats   38
   Prioritization   38
   Strengthening Incident Response With Security Intelligence   38
SecOps Intelligence in Action   39
   Use case: Prepare processes in advance   39
   Use case: Scope and contain incidents   40
   Use case: Detect data breaches sooner   41
   Abuse case: Half measures are worse than nothing   41
Essential Characteristics of Security Intelligence for Incident Response   42
   Comprehensive   42
   Relevant   43
   Contextualized   44
   Integrated   45

Chapter 6: Vulnerability Intelligence   47

The Vulnerability Problem by the Numbers   48
   Zero day does not mean top priority   48
   Time is of the essence   48
Assess Risk Based on Exploitability   49
   Severity ratings are often misleading   50
The Genesis of Security Intelligence: Vulnerability Databases   51
   Exploitability versus exploitation   51
   Next week versus now   53
Vulnerability Intelligence and Real Risk   54
   Internal vulnerability scanning   54
   Risk milestones for vulnerabilities   54
   Understanding the adversary   55
Sources of Intelligence   56
Use Cases for Cross-Referencing Intelligence   58
Bridging the Risk Gaps Among Security, Operations, and Business Leadership   58

Chapter 7: Threat Intelligence Part 1 – Knowing Attackers   61

Threat Intelligence as Part of Security Intelligence   61
Understand Your Enemy   62
Criminal Communities and the Dark Web   64
   Gated communities   65
   A strength — and a weakness   65
Connecting the Dots   66
Use Case: More Comprehensive Incident Response   67
Use Case: Proactive Threat Hunting   67
Use Case: Advance Warning of Payment Fraud   68

Chapter 8: Threat Intelligence Part 2 – Risk Analysis — 71
- The FAIR Risk Model — 72
  - Measurements and transparency are key — 73
- Security Intelligence and Threat Probabilities — 74
- Security Intelligence and the Financial Cost of Attacks — 76

Chapter 9: Third-Party Intelligence — 79
- Third-Party Risk Looms Large — 79
- Traditional Risk Assessments Fall Short — 81
- Three Things to Look for in Security Intelligence — 82
  - Automation and analytics — 82
  - Real-time updates to risk scores — 83
  - Transparent risk assessments — 84
- Responding to High Third-Party Risk Scores — 86

Chapter 10: Brand Intelligence — 89
- Protect Your Brand and Your Customers — 90
- A Different Kind of Detection — 90
- Uncovering Evidence of Brand Impersonation and Abuse — 91
  - Use case: Typosquatting and fraudulent domains — 91
- Uncovering Evidence of Breaches on the Web — 92
  - Use case: Compromised data — 93
- Critical Qualities for Security Intelligence Solutions — 95

Chapter 11: Geopolitical Intelligence — 97
- What Is Geopolitical Risk? — 97
- Geopolitical Intelligence — 98
  - Location, location, location — 99
  - Supply chains, customers, and geopolitical risk — 99
- Who Uses Geopolitical Intelligence? — 99
- Data Collection With Geofencing — 100
- Data and Information Sources — 101
- Automation, Analytics, and Expertise — 102
- Interacting With Geopolitical Intelligence — 104
- Geopolitics and Cyber Threats — 105

Chapter 12: Security Intelligence for Security Leaders — 107
- Risk Management — 108
  - Internal data is not enough — 108
  - Sharpening the focus — 109
- Mitigation: People, Processes, and Tools — 110
  - Early warnings — 111
- Investment — 111
- Communication — 112
- Supporting Security Leaders — 113
- The Security Skills Gap — 114

Section 3: Creating and Scaling Your Security Intelligence Program

Chapter 13: Analytical Frameworks for Security Intelligence — 119
The Lockheed Martin Cyber Kill Chain® — 120
    Limitations of the Cyber Kill Chain — 121
The Diamond Model — 122
    Flexibility — 123
    Drawbacks of the Diamond Model — 123
The MITRE ATT&CK™ Framework — 124
    Categories of attacker behavior — 125

Chapter 14: Your Security Intelligence Journey — 127
Don't Start With Threat Feeds — 127
Clarify Your Security Intelligence Needs and Goals — 128
    Answer these questions — 128
    Identify which of your teams will benefit from security intelligence — 128
Key Success Factors — 129
    Generating quick wins with monitoring — 129
    Ensuring that reports are useful — 130
    Automating as much as possible — 130
    Integrating security intelligence with processes and infrastructure — 131
    Getting experts to nurture internal experts — 132
Start Simple and Scale Up — 132

Chapter 15: Developing Your Core Security Intelligence Team — 135
Dedicated, but Not Necessarily Separate — 135
    A dedicated team is best — 136
    Where the team sits depends on your organization — 136
Core Competencies — 138
Collecting and Enriching Threat Data — 139
    The human edge — 139
    Additional sources — 139
    Combining sources — 139
    The role of intelligent machines — 140
Engaging With Security Intelligence Communities — 141

Conclusion: Using Elite Intelligence to Disrupt Adversaries — 143
Key Takeaways From the Book — 143

Foreword to the Third Edition

At the end of 2019, I came to two realizations...

The first: There has never been a better time to be a cybercriminal.

The second: Only teams of defenders that are focused on proactively disrupting adversaries will win.

In the months that followed, both theories have proven to be correct.

Anyone with a desire to do harm can put an organization's most sensitive data at risk by purchasing off-the-shelf tools and easily accessing underground, illicit marketplaces.

Legacy vulnerabilities, lack of secure code development processes, explosive growth of connected devices, and the absolute decimation of organizational perimeters have put security teams on their heels — if they're still on their feet at all.

In March of 2020, the COVID-19 pandemic forced organizations to send home their workforces for months on end, with little-to-no ability to implement security controls from afar. To make matters more complicated, there are no government bodies — no unified front — protecting the interests of organizations against threat actors, from your run-of-the-mill bad guys to nation-state attackers.

So, how do your security teams survive and continue to defend your organization in times like these?

Security intelligence is an outcomes-centric approach to reducing risk that fuses internal and external threat, security, and business insights across an entire organization. It easily scales up and down to match the organization's size, maturity, and specific needs. At Recorded Future, our ability to collect, structure, analyze, and deliver all relevant security information on the internet is what has set us apart since the very beginning. We've now taken that ability and segmented it to meet the specific needs of each security solution.

In September of 2020, Recorded Future announced the tailoring of our Security Intelligence Platform to meet the intelligence challenges across every security function. Providing a single authoritative source for intelligence, the six individual modules we provide deliver actionable, customized intelligence that enables users to stay nimble and precise in their security decision-making. Based on their role, target use cases, and focused outcomes, these solutions include the Brand Intelligence Module, SecOps Intelligence Module, Threat Intelligence Module, Vulnerability Intelligence Module, Third-Party Intelligence Module, and Geopolitical Intelligence Module.

Geopolitical intelligence is the latest innovation to be added to the Recorded Future Security Intelligence Platform. This solution accelerates critical decision-making with contextual open-source intelligence (OSINT) on geopolitical threats and trends — empowering users to protect assets and understand shifting dynamics in the geographic areas relevant to their organizations. Eliminating manual research and surfacing intelligence in real time enables users to defend assets anywhere in the world with a comprehensive view of their organization's cyber and physical threat landscape.

In late 2019, we introduced the three principles of effective security intelligence. In 2020, we added a fourth. It has quickly moved to number one on our list:

1. You must focus on disrupting the adversaries most likely to target you — and make their lives as challenging as possible. Security intelligence is the most effective way to do this.

2. Security intelligence must provide the timely, clear, and actionable context required to make fast, informed decisions and take effective action as it applies to each security challenge. Intelligence has to come at the right time, in a form that is understandable, and it must amplify the impact of existing solutions. It needs to enrich your knowledge, not complicate the decision-making process, and it must put everybody in your organization on the same page.

3. People and machines work better together. Machines are capable of processing and categorizing raw data exponentially faster than humans. On the other hand, humans are much better equipped to perform intuitive, big-picture analysis than any artificial intelligence — as long as they're not overwhelmed with sorting through huge data sets and performing endless research. When people and machines are paired, each works smarter, saving time and money, reducing human burnout, and improving security overall.

4. Security intelligence is for everyone. No matter what security role you play, intelligence enables better, faster decisions. It's not a separate domain of security — it's the context that empowers you to work smarter, whether you're staffing a SOC, managing vulnerabilities, or making high-level business decisions. To make things easier, not harder, effective security intelligence must integrate with the solutions and workflows on which you already rely — and it has to be easy to implement.

At Recorded Future, we believe wholeheartedly in these core principles, and our approach has been validated in the years since the first edition of this handbook was released. Our intelligence is stopping threats in the security departments of 99 of the *Fortune* 100 top companies in the United States — not to mention countless organizations of all sizes, as well as government institutions around the world. And we've grown to more than 500 employees from 40 countries.

We hope this handbook will play its part by offering practical information and advice that you can apply today to disrupt the adversaries your organization faces.

I am grateful to everyone who has contributed to the contents of this handbook: Our users and clients, industry experts, and the Recorded Future team. Hopefully you will find this third edition of our handbook to be an informative companion as you integrate security intelligence across your security ecosystem.

Christopher Ahlberg, Ph.D.
Co-Founder and CEO
Recorded Future

Introduction

A Complete Picture of Security Intelligence

Like the blind people surveying the elephant in the fable, most people have only a limited understanding of security intelligence because they have only come into contact with one aspect of it.

You might have heard that security intelligence involves collecting data from a wide variety of sources, including the dark web. You may know that it combines that data with insights from cybersecurity experts, and distills the data and insights into intelligence for IT security professionals. You might work with threat feeds or weekly reports about attacks on the network, or even expert analysis of cyber risks. However, it's unlikely that you entirely appreciate the wide range of roles and functions that security intelligence supports, all of the ways it protects organizations and their assets, or its full potential for reducing risk.

This handbook will give you a complete picture of the elephant. The beginning provides an overview of security intelligence and the phases of the security intelligence lifecycle. The middle of the book examines the specific ways that security intelligence strengthens six critical security functions and their workflows. The final chapters deal with management and implementation issues, like using security intelligence to evaluate risk and justify investments, and how to build a security intelligence team.

By the end, you will understand how security intelligence amplifies the effectiveness of security teams and security leaders by exposing unknown threats, clarifying priorities, providing data to make better, faster decisions, and driving a common understanding of risk reduction across the organization.

From Threat Intelligence to Security Intelligence

Until recently, the topics discussed in this book were commonly known as "threat intelligence." In fact, the previous release was titled *The Threat Intelligence Handbook, Second Edition*.

However, the term "threat intelligence" is generally associated with information about threats to traditional IT systems controlled by the organization. This conception of the field is far too narrow.

Innovative threat actors continuously probe for weak points and develop new ways to penetrate or circumvent traditional IT defenses. They steal credentials from trusted third parties and use those to burrow into corporate systems. They harvest personal information from social media platforms to produce convincing phishing campaigns, and create typosquatting websites to impersonate brands and defraud customers. They plot cyberattacks and leverage physical events against remote facilities around the world. They devise attacks that, without prior warning, are undetectable by conventional IT security solutions.

Forward-thinking cybersecurity experts and IT groups have realized that they need to take the battle to the threat actors by uncovering their methods and disrupting their activities before they attack. This realization has prompted them to expand their intelligence programs to include areas such as third-party risk (exposure through vendors, suppliers, and business partners), brand protection (the ability to detect and resolve security issues that threaten an organization's reputation), geopolitical risk (threats associated with the locations of physical assets and events), and more.

Now, experts and vendors are using the term "security intelligence" to encompass everything that was previously called "threat intelligence," as well as the newer areas of the field. That is why the book you're reading right now is titled *The Security Intelligence Handbook*.

You may also notice that we have revised and reorganized material from earlier editions to align with the concept of security intelligence. For instance, we:

- Sharpened our focus on how security intelligence strengths six major security functions
- Explored new use cases and examples of ways to utilize security intelligence for activities such as incident response and proactive threat hunting
- Expanded the discussion of brand protection
- Added a new chapter on geopolitical risk
- Added a discussion of how to use a Threat Category Risk (TCR) framework to quantify threats based on monetary impact to an organization

We hope this handbook will empower you to disrupt adversaries and reduce your organization's risk — or at the very least, stimulate new ways of thinking about what it means to be a defender in the current landscape.

— The Recorded Future Team

Chapters at a Glance

Section 1: What Is Security Intelligence?

Chapter 1, "What Is Security Intelligence," outlines the value of security intelligence and the characteristics of successful security intelligence programs.

Chapter 2, "Types and Sources," discusses the differences between operational and strategic security intelligence, as well as the roles of data feeds and the dark web.

Chapter 3, "The Security Intelligence Lifecycle," examines the phases of the security intelligence lifecycle and the relationship between tools and human analysts.

Section 2: Applications of Security Intelligence

Chapter 4, "SecOps Intelligence Part 1: Triage," explores how intelligence provides context for triage and enables security operations teams to make better, faster decisions.

Chapter 5, "SecOps Intelligence Part 2: Response," discusses how intelligence minimizes reactivity in incident response and presents four use cases.

Chapter 6, "Vulnerability Intelligence," examines how intelligence enables practitioners to prioritize vulnerabilities based on true risk to the organization.

Chapter 7, "Threat Intelligence Part 1: Understanding Attackers," explains the value of researching attacker tactics, techniques, and procedures (TTPs).

Chapter 8, "Threat Intelligence Part 2: Risk Analysis," analyzes the value of risk models and how security intelligence provides hard data about attack probabilities and costs.

Chapter 9, "Third-Party Intelligence," explores how intelligence is used to assess supply-chain partners and reduce third-party risk.

Chapter 10, "Brand Intelligence," reviews different forms of digital risks to brands and how security intelligence empowers security teams to defend their organization's reputation.

Chapter 11, "Geopolitical Intelligence," describes how security intelligence provides advanced warning of threats to facilities and physical assets around the world.

Chapter 12, "Security Intelligence for Security Leaders," examines how security intelligence enables CISOs, CIOs, and other leaders to obtain a holistic view of the cyber risk landscape and make better business decisions.

Section 3: Creating and Scaling Your Security Intelligence Program

Chapter 13, "Analytical Frameworks for Security Intelligence," explains how three leading threat frameworks provide useful structures for thinking about attacks.

Chapter 14, "Your Security Intelligence Journey," provides suggestions on how to start simple and scale up a security intelligence program.

Chapter 15, "Developing Your Core Security Intelligence Team," describes how building a dedicated team takes security intelligence to a new level.

Helpful Icons

Tips provide practical advice you may want to apply in your own organization.

When you see this icon, take note, as the related content contains key information that you'll want to remember.

Proceed with caution because it may prove costly to you and your organization if you don't.

Content associated with this icon is more technical in nature and is intended for IT and security practitioners.

Want to learn more? Find related content online.

Section 1: What Is Security Intelligence?

Chapter 1

What Is Security Intelligence?

In this chapter

- Understand why security intelligence is important
- Review characteristics of successful security intelligence programs
- Learn who benefits from using security intelligence

"Every battle is won before it is ever fought."
— Sun Tzu

Visibility Into Threats Before They Strike

Cyber threats come in many forms. Certainly some of them are cybercriminals who attack your network at the firewall. However, they also include threat actors operating on the open and dark web who come at you through your employees and your business partners. Some devastate your brand through social media and external websites without ever touching your network. Malicious or merely careless insiders may also wreak havoc with your data and your reputation.

By the time you see indicators of these threats on your network, it is probably too late. To prevent damage, you need advance warning of threats, accompanied by actionable facts in order to:

☑ Eliminate your most serious vulnerabilities before they are exploited

- ☑ Detect probes and attacks at the earliest possible moment and respond effectively right away
- ☑ Understand the tactics, techniques, and procedures (TTPs) of likely attackers and put effective defenses in place
- ☑ Identify and correct your business partners' security weaknesses — especially those that have access to your network
- ☑ Detect data leaks and impersonations of your corporate brand
- ☑ Make wise investments in security to maximize return and minimize risk

Many IT organizations have created intelligence programs to obtain the advance warning and actionable facts they need to protect their data and their brands. Figure 1-1 lists metrics that show the dramatic improvement in security and efficiency that a security intelligence program provides.

Topline Metrics

Overall more efficient IT security teams	3-year ROI	To payback
32%	**284%**	**4 Months**

Security Operational Efficiencies

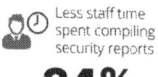

Less staff time spent compiling security reports	Earlier identification of threats	Faster resolution of security threats
34%	**10x**	**63%**

Risk Reduction

22%	86%	$1M
More security threats identified before impact	Reduction in unplanned downtime	Potential penalties/fines per breach avoided

Figure 1-1: A security intelligence program can produce dramatic improvements in security and efficiency. Source of data: IDC

Actionable Facts and Insights

When people speak of security intelligence, sometimes they are referring to certain types of facts and insights, and other times to the process that produces them. Let's look at the first case.

More than data or information

Even security professionals sometimes use the words "data," "information" and "intelligence" interchangeably, but the distinctions are important. Figure 1-2 highlights these differences.

Data consists of discrete facts and statistics gathered as the basis for further analysis.

Information is comprised of multiple data points that are combined to answer specific questions.

Intelligence is the output of an analysis of data and information that uncovers patterns and provides vital context to inform decision-making.

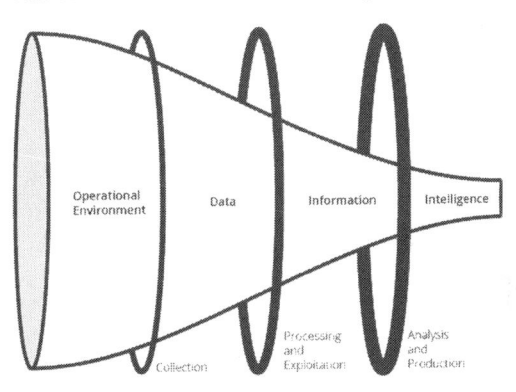

Figure 1-2: The relationship between data, information, and intelligence.

Of course, the details of the data, information, and intelligence differ across political, military, economic, business, and other types of intelligence programs. For security intelligence:

- ☑ Data is usually just indicators such as IP addresses, URLs, or hashes. Data doesn't tell us much without analysis.

- ☑ Information answers questions like, "How many times has my organization been mentioned on social media this month?" Although this is a far more useful output than the raw data, it still doesn't directly inform a specific action.

- ☑ Intelligence is factual insight based on analysis that correlates data and information from across different sources to uncover patterns and add insights. It enables people and systems to make informed decisions and take effective action to prevent breaches, remediate vulnerabilities, improve the organization's security posture, and reduce risk.

Implicit in this definition of "intelligence" is the idea that every instance of security intelligence is *actionable* for a *specific audience*. That is, intelligence must do two things:

1. Point toward specific decisions or actions
2. Be tailored for easy use by a specific person, group, or system that will use it to make a decision or take an action

Data feeds that are never used and reports that are never read are not intelligence. Neither is information, no matter how accurate or insightful, if it is provided to someone who can't interpret it correctly or isn't in a position to act on it.

Security Intelligence: The Process

Security intelligence also refers to the process by which data and information are collected, analyzed, and disseminated throughout the organization. The steps in such a process will be discussed in Chapter 3, where we describe the security intelligence lifecycle. However, it is important to note at the outset that successful security intelligence processes have four characteristics.

1. A collaborative process and framework

In many organizations, security intelligence efforts are siloed. For example, the security operations (SecOps), fraud prevention, and third-party risk teams may have their own analysts and tools for gathering and analyzing intelligence. This leads to waste, duplication, and an inability to share analysis and intelligence. Silos also make it impossible to assess risk across the organization and to direct security resources where they will have the greatest impact. Security intelligence programs need to share a common process and framework, enable broad access to insights and operational workflows, encourage a "big picture" view of risk, and account for the allocation of resources.

2. 360-degree visibility

Because cyber threats may come from anywhere, security intelligence programs need visibility everywhere, including:

- ☑ Security events on the corporate network
- ☑ Conventional threat data feeds
- ☑ Open web forums where attackers exchange information and tools for exploiting vulnerabilities
- ☑ Dark web communities where hackers and state-sponsored actors share techniques and plot attacks
- ☑ Online marketplaces where cybercriminals buy and sell confidential information
- ☑ Social media accounts where threat actors impersonate your employees and counterfeit your products

Today, many organizations focus on conventional threat data feeds, and are only now becoming aware of the need to scan a broader variety and greater quantity of sources on a regular basis.

3. Extensive automation and integration

Because there is so much data and information to capture, correlate, and process, a security intelligence program needs a high degree of automation to reduce manual efforts and produce meaningful results quickly. To add context to initial findings and effectively disseminate intelligence, successful security intelligence programs must also integrate with many types of security solutions, such as security dashboards, security information and event management solutions (SIEMs), vulnerability management systems, firewalls, and security orchestration, automation and response (SOAR) tools.

4. Alignment with the organization and security use cases

Organizations sometimes waste enormous resources capturing and analyzing information that isn't relevant to them. A successful security intelligence program needs to determine and document its intelligence needs to ensure that collection and processing activities align with the organization's actual priorities. Alignment also means tailoring the content and format of intelligence to make it easy for people and systems to use.

Who Benefits From Security Intelligence?

Security intelligence is sometimes perceived to be simply a research service for the security operations and incident response teams, or the domain of elite analysts. In reality, it adds value to every security function and to several other teams in the organization.

The middle section of this handbook examines the primary use cases:

- ☑ **Security operations and incident response teams** are routinely overwhelmed by alerts. Security intelligence accelerates their alert triage, minimizes false positives, provides context for better decision-making, and empowers them to respond faster.

- ☑ **Vulnerability management teams** often struggle to differentiate between relevant, critical vulnerabilities and those that are unimportant to their organization. Security intelligence delivers context and risk scoring that enables them to reduce downtime while patching the vulnerabilities that really matter first.

- ☑ **Threat analysts** need to understand the motives and TTPs of threat actors and track security trends for industries, technologies, and regions. Security intelligence provides them with deeper and more-expansive knowledge to generate more valuable insights.

- ☑ **Third-party risk programs** need up-to-date information on the security postures of vendors, suppliers, and other third parties that access the organization's systems. Security intelligence arms them with an ongoing flow of objective, detailed information about business partners that static vendor questionnaires and traditional procurement methods can't offer.

- ☑ **Brand protection teams** need continuous visibility into unsanctioned web and social media mentions, data leaks, employee impersonations, counterfeit products, typosquatting websites, phishing attacks, and more. Security intelligence tools monitor for these across the internet at scale, and streamline takedown and remediation processes.

- ☑ **Geopolitical risk and physical security teams** rely on advanced warning of attacks, protests, and other threats to assets in locations around the globe. Security intelligence programs capture data and "chatter" from multiple sources and filter it to deliver precise intelligence about what's happening in the cities, countries, and regions of interest.

- ☑ **Security leaders** use intelligence about likely threats and their potential business impact to assess security requirements, quantify risks (ideally in monetary terms), develop mitigation strategies, and justify cybersecurity investments to CEOs, CFOs, and board members.

ON THE WEB

For a concise introduction to security intelligence and six critical solution areas, read the Recorded Future white paper, "Security Intelligence: Driving Security From Analytics to Action."

Chapter 2

Types and Sources

In this chapter

- Differentiate between operational and strategic security intelligence
- Appreciate the roles of data feeds, private channels, and the dark web

"It is a very sad thing that nowadays there is so little useless information."

— Oscar Wilde

Two Types of Security Intelligence

Security intelligence is a broad concept that is actually made up of two kinds of intelligence — **operational** and **strategic**. These two types of intelligence differ in their sources, the audiences they serve, and the formats in which they appear.

The purpose in making this distinction is recognizing that the various security teams have different goals and degrees of technical knowledge. As we said earlier, intelligence needs to be actionable — but because the responsibilities of a vulnerability management team differ significantly from those of a CISO, "actionability" has distinct implications for each, and the form and content of the intelligence they'll benefit from the most will vary.

Operational security intelligence

Operational security intelligence is knowledge about ongoing cyberattacks, events, and campaigns. It provides specialized insights that enable the individuals that use it to understand the nature, intent, and timing of specific attacks as they are occurring. It's generally sourced from machines.

Operational intelligence is sometimes referred to as **technical security intelligence** or **technical threat intelligence**, because it usually includes technical information about attacks, such as which attack vectors are being used, what vulnerabilities are being exploited, and what command and control domains are being employed by attackers. This kind of intelligence is often most useful to personnel directly involved in the defense of an organization, such as system architects, administrators, and security staff.

Threat data feeds are often used to inform technical information. These feeds usually focus on a single type of threat indicator, such as malware hashes or suspicious domains. As we discuss below, threat data feeds supply input for security intelligence, but the data points they provide are not security intelligence.

> **TIP** Operational security intelligence is commonly used to guide improvements to existing security controls and processes, and to speed up incident response. An operational intelligence solution that integrates with data from your network is crucial because it answers urgent questions unique to your organization, such as, "Is this critical vulnerability, which is being exploited in my industry, present in my systems?"

Strategic security intelligence

Strategic security intelligence provides a broad overview of an organization's entire threat landscape. It's most useful for informing high-level decisions by executives. The content is generally business oriented and presented through reports or briefings. Machines aren't capable of generating these materials — they must be created by humans with expertise.

This kind of intelligence requires human interaction because it takes analytical thought to evaluate and test new adversary TTPs against existing security controls. Pieces of this process may be automated, but a human mind is required to complete the exercise.

Good strategic intelligence must provide insight into the risks associated with certain actions, broad patterns in threat actor tactics and targets, geopolitical events and trends, and similar topics.

Common strategic security intelligence sources include:

- ☑ Policy documents from nation-states or non-governmental organizations
- ☑ News from local and national media, articles in industry- and subject-specific publications, and input from subject-matter experts
- ☑ White papers, research reports, and other content produced by security organizations

Organizations must set strategic security intelligence requirements by asking focused, specific questions. Analysts with expertise outside of typical cybersecurity skills — in particular, a strong understanding of sociopolitical and business concepts — are needed to gather and interpret strategic security intelligence.

DON'T FORGET

Some aspects of the production of strategic security intelligence need to be automated. Even when the final product is non-technical, producing effective strategic security intelligence takes deep research on massive volumes of data, often across multiple languages. These challenges make initial data collection and processing too difficult to perform manually, even for those rare analysts who possess the right language skills, technical background, and tradecraft. A security intelligence solution that automates data collection and processing reduces this burden and enables analysts with various levels of expertise to work more effectively.

The Role of Threat Data Feeds

We mentioned earlier that data is not intelligence, and that threat data feeds often overwhelm analysts already burdened with countless daily alerts and notifications. However, when used correctly, threat data feeds provide valuable raw material for security intelligence.

Threat data feeds are real-time streams of data that provide information on potential cyber threats and risks. They're usually lists of simple indicators or artifacts focused on a single area of interest, like suspicious domains, hashes, bad IPs, or malicious code. They provide a quick, real-time look at the threat landscape.

CAUTION: Many feeds are filled with errors, redundancies, and false positives. These create confusion and extra work, so it's critical to select high-quality data feeds.

Evaluating Threat Data Feeds

Use these criteria to assess threat data feeds for your organization:

Data sources: Feeds pull their data from all kinds of sources — many of which are not relevant to your organization. For example, you will get the most value from data gathered from organizations in your industry.

Transparency of sources: Knowing where your data is coming from empowers you to evaluate its relevance and usefulness.

Percentage of unique data: Some paid feeds just aggregate data from other feeds, and often list the same items several times.

Periodicity of data: Data should be collected frequently, and should cover the time period relevant to your organization. Also, it should cover a long enough timespan to support strategic intelligence on long-term trends.

Measurable outcomes: Being able to track the correlation rate — the percentage of alerts that correspond with your internal telemetry in a given week, month, or quarter — is critical to calculating the measurable outcomes of a particular feed.

TIP: Instead of viewing dozens of feeds separately, use a security intelligence platform that combines them all into a single feed, removes duplicates and false positives, compares them with internal telemetry, and generates prioritized alerts. The most powerful security intelligence platforms even allow organizations to create custom security intelligence feeds, or curate and set up automated alerting.

The Role of Private Channels and the Dark Web

Threat data feeds and publicly available information are not the only external data sources for security intelligence. Vital operational and strategic intelligence on specific attacks, attacker TTPs, political goals of hacktivists and state actors, and other key topics can be gathered by infiltrating or breaking into private channels of communication used by threat groups. These include encrypted messaging apps, exclusive forums on the dark web, and other sources.

However, there are barriers to gathering this kind of intelligence:

- ☑ **Access**: Threat groups may communicate over private and encrypted channels, or require proof of identification or an invitation from an administrator.
- ☑ **Language**: Activity on forums is carried out in Russian, Chinese, Indonesian, Arabic, and many other languages — and slang and specialized jargon are used regularly.
- ☑ **Noise**: High volumes of conversation make it difficult or impossible to manually gather good intelligence from sources like chat rooms and social media.
- ☑ **Obfuscation**: To avoid detection, many threat groups employ obfuscation tactics like using codenames.

Overcoming these barriers requires a large investment in tools and expertise for monitoring private channels — or a security intelligence service provider that has already made that investment.

TIP Look for security intelligence solutions and services that employ algorithms and analytical processes for automated data collection on a large scale. A solution that uses natural language processing, for example, will be able to gather information from foreign-language sources without needing human expertise to decipher it.

Chapter 3

The Security Intelligence Lifecycle

In this chapter

- Examine the phases of the security intelligence lifecycle
- Review sources of security intelligence
- Explore the roles of security intelligence tools and human analysts

"You have to believe in your process."
— Tom Brady

The Six Phases of the Security Intelligence Lifecycle

Security intelligence is built on analytic techniques honed over several decades by government and military agencies. There are six distinct phases that make up what is called the "intelligence cycle":

1. Direction
2. Collection
3. Processing
4. Analysis
5. Dissemination
6. Feedback

Figure 3-1 shows how those six phases align with security intelligence.

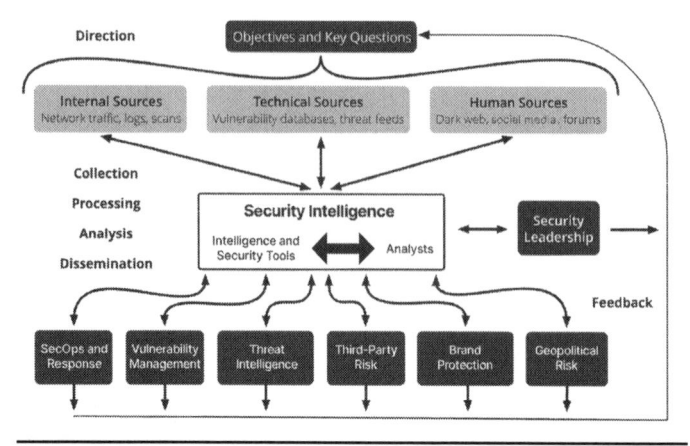

Figure 3-1: Security intelligence and the six phases of the intelligence cycle.

Direction

The direction phase of the security intelligence lifecycle is when you set the goals for your security intelligence program. This involves understanding and articulating:

- ☑ The information assets and business processes that need to be protected
- ☑ The potential impacts of losing those assets or interrupting those processes
- ☑ The types of security intelligence that your organization requires to protect assets and respond to threats
- ☑ The priorities about what you need to protect

Once high-level intelligence needs are determined, an organization is able to formulate questions that channel the need for information into discrete requirements. For example, if a goal is to understand likely adversaries, one logical question would be, "Which threat actors on underground forums are actively soliciting data concerning our organization?"

> **A Library of Goals**
>
> Recorded Future has created a list of pre-configured intelligence goals that includes the most common intelligence requirements of the *Fortune* Global 500 organizations. This list enables companies that are new to security intelligence to think about their issues and priorities and decide how to plug security intelligence into their existing processes. To learn more about the Intelligence Goals Library, go to https://www.recordedfuture.com/intelligence-goals-library-overview/.
>
> Adversarial models such as the Lockheed-Martin Cyber Kill Chain® and the MITRE Adversarial Tactics, Techniques & Common Knowledge (ATT&CK™) matrix (discussed in Chapter 13), may also assist companies in focusing on the types of security intelligence they need to prevent breaches and reduce risk.

Collection

Collection is the process of gathering information to address the most important intelligence requirements. It can occur organically through a variety of means, including:

- ☑ Pulling metadata and logs from internal networks and security devices
- ☑ Subscribing to threat data feeds from industry organizations and cybersecurity vendors
- ☑ Conducting conversations and targeted interviews with knowledgeable sources
- ☑ Scanning news websites and blogs
- ☑ Scanning social media platforms
- ☑ Scraping and harvesting websites and forums
- ☑ Infiltrating closed sources, such as dark web forums

The data collected typically will be a combination of finished information, such as intelligence reports from cybersecurity experts and vendors, and raw data, like malware signatures or leaked credentials on a paste site.

> ## Security Intelligence Sources
>
> **Technical sources** (e.g., threat feeds): These are available in huge quantities, often for free. Technical sources are easy to integrate with existing security technologies, but they often contain a high proportion of false positives and outdated results.
>
> **Media** (e.g., security websites, vendor research): These sources often provide useful information about emerging threats, but they are hard to connect with technical indicators to measure risk.
>
> **Social media**: Social channels offer huge amounts of valuable data, but it comes at a price. False positives and misinformation are rampant, so a tremendous amount of cross-referencing with other sources is required to determine which insights are usable.
>
> **Threat actor forums**: Specifically designed to host discussions about cyberattacks, these forums offer some of the most actionable insights available anywhere. Once again, however, analysis and cross-referencing are essential to determine what is truly valuable.
>
> **The dark web** (including markets and forums): While often the birthplace of hugely valuable intelligence, dark web sources may be extremely difficult to access — particularly those that play host to serious criminal communities.

DON'T FORGET You need multiple sources of intelligence to form a complete picture of potential and actual threats. As shown in Figure 3-1, these include:

- ☑ **Internal sources** like firewall and router logs, network packet capture tools, and vulnerability scans
- ☑ **Technical sources** such as vulnerability databases and threat data feeds
- ☑ **Human sources** including traditional and social media, cybersecurity forums and blogs, and dark web forums

Missing any one of these may slow down investigations and cause gaps in remediation.

TIP Automate! Analysts should spend as little time as possible collecting data, and as much time as possible evaluating and communicating threat information.

Processing

Processing is the transformation of collected information into a format usable by the organization. Almost all raw data collected needs to be processed in some manner, whether by humans or machines.

Different collection methods often require different means of processing. Human reports may need to be correlated and ranked, deconflicted, and checked. An example might be extracting IP addresses from a security vendor's report and adding them to a CSV file for importing to a SIEM product. In a more technical area, processing might involve extracting indicators from an email, enriching them with other information, and then communicating with endpoint protection tools for automated blocking.

TIP Automate more! The right tools will enable you to automate most processing workflows and collection processes. For example, a security automation tool might identify a suspicious indicator of compromise (IOC), then conduct a sequence of checks to bring context to the IOC. This saves the analyst valuable time that would otherwise need to be spent performing those checks manually.

ON THE WEB To learn more about how automation enhances security intelligence, read the short Recorded Future e-book, "Beyond SOAR: 5 Ways to Automate Security With Intelligence."

Analysis

Analysis is the process of turning information into intelligence to inform decisions. Depending on the circumstances, these decisions might involve whether to investigate a potential threat, what actions to take immediately to block an attack, how to strengthen security controls, or how much investment in additional security resources is justified. Analysis is generally performed either by a human or a very sophisticated algorithm.

DON'T FORGET Analysts must have a clear understanding of who is going to be using their intelligence and what decisions those people make. The intelligence they deliver needs to be perceived as actionable, not as academic. Most of this book is devoted to giving you a clear picture of exactly how security intelligence improves decision-making and actions in different areas of security.

The form in which the information is presented is especially important. It is useless and wasteful to collect and process information only to deliver it in a form that can't be understood and used by the decision maker.

For example, if you want to communicate with non-technical leaders, your report must:

- ☑ Be concise (a one-page memo or a handful of slides)
- ☑ Avoid confusing and overly technical terms and jargon
- ☑ Articulate the issues in business terms (such as direct and indirect costs and impact on reputation)
- ☑ Include a recommended course of action

Some intelligence may need to be delivered in a variety of formats for different audiences, like a live video feed and a written brief. Not all intelligence needs to be digested via a formal report. Successful security intelligence teams provide continual technical reporting to other security teams with external context around IOCs, malware, threat actors, vulnerabilities, and threat trends.

Dissemination

Dissemination involves getting the finished intelligence output to the places it needs to go.

As illustrated in Figure 3-1, most cybersecurity organizations have at least six teams plus security leaders who benefit from security intelligence. For each of these audiences, you need to ask:

- What security intelligence do they need, and how does external information best support their activities?
- How should the intelligence be selected and organized to make it easily understandable and actionable for that audience?
- How often should we provide updates and other information?

- Through what media (emails, newsletters, web forums, documents, slides, oral presentations) should the intelligence be disseminated?
- How should we follow up if they have questions?

Feedback

Regular input is required to understand the requirements of each group and make adjustments as their requirements and priorities change. That input is gathered in the feedback phase. It is critically important to understand your overall intelligence priorities and the requirements of your "customers" — the security teams that consume the security intelligence. Their needs guide all phases of the lifecycle and tell you:

- ☑ What types of data to collect
- ☑ How to process and enrich the data to turn it into useful information
- ☑ How to analyze the information and present it as actionable intelligence
- ☑ To whom each type of intelligence must be disseminated, how quickly it needs to be disseminated, and how fast to respond to questions

TIP For every "customer" team, establish channels for both fast, informal feedback (such as an email address, an internal forum, or a team collaboration tool), and a formal, structured process (such as an online survey or a quarterly face-to-face meeting). The informal channel enables you to react and adjust immediately, while the structured process ensures that you get input from everyone and are able to track your progress over time.

Tools and People

Tools are essential to automating the collection, processing, and dissemination steps in the intelligence lifecycle — and to supporting and accelerating analysis. Without the right tools, analysts will spend all their time on the mechanical aspects of these tasks and never have time for analysis.

Most mature security intelligence groups leverage two types of tools:

- ☑ A security intelligence solution designed to collect, process, and analyze all types of threat data from internal, technical, and human sources
- ☑ Existing security tools, such as SIEMs and security analytics, which collect and correlate security events and log data

Human analysts are equally important — if not more important. You can't rely on tools to interview security experts and probe closed dark web forums. Also, you need people to analyze and synthesize intelligence for the security teams and managers who will consume it.

The analysts do not need to belong to a central, elite intelligence department. Someone does need to take an organization-wide view of the security intelligence function, make decisions about resources and priorities, and track progress, but success is achievable under a variety of organizational structures. You could have a central group with dedicated security intelligence analysts, or a small group inside the security operations and incident response organization. Alternatively, members of the different cybersecurity groups may be responsible for analyzing security intelligence for their direct colleagues.

In Chapter 14, we discuss how the organizational structure often evolves as the security intelligence function matures, and Chapter 15 provides advice on how to organize a core security intelligence team.

Section 2: Applications of Security Intelligence

Chapter 4

SecOps Intelligence Part 1 – Triage

In this chapter

- See how "alert fatigue" risks undoing the good work of SecOps teams
- Understand the value of context for improving triage
- Learn how security intelligence reduces wasted time and improves triage decisions

"Being the worst makes you first."

— Sign in hospital emergency room

Triage is a critical but exhausting job for security operations teams. They find themselves held hostage to the huge volumes of alerts generated by the networks they monitor. According to the Ponemon "Cost of Malware Containment" report, security teams can expect to log nearly 17,000 malware alerts in a typical week. That's more than 100 alerts per hour for a team that operates 24/7. And those are only the alerts from malware incidents. To put these figures in perspective, all these alerts can force security teams to spend more 21,000 man-hours each year chasing down false positives. That's 2,625 standard eight-hour shifts needed just to distinguish bad alerts from good ones.

Let's examine how security intelligence mitigates this overload by filtering out false alarms, speeding up analysis of alerts, and providing context to make better triage decisions.

Responsibilities of the SecOps Team

On paper, the responsibilities of the SecOps team seem simple:

- ☑ Monitor for potential threats
- ☑ Detect suspicious network activity
- ☑ Contain active threats
- ☑ Remediate threats using available technology

When a suspicious event is detected, the SecOps team investigates it, then works with other security teams to reduce the impact and severity of the attack. Think of the roles and responsibilities of SecOps as similar to those of emergency services teams responding to 911 calls, as shown in Figure 4-1.

Stage	Role	Responsibilities
Triage	Operator (911 Center) Security Analyst (SOC)	Determine the relevance and urgency of each incoming alert. Decide if the alert is legitimate and should be escalated.
First Response	First Responder (911) Incident Responder (SOC)	Determine the scope of the incident. Identify affected and vulnerable systems. Recommend actions to contain the effects.
Investigation	Detective (911) Threat Hunter (SOC)	Determine root causes and weaknesses in defenses. Recommend actions to prevent recurrences.

Figure 4-1: The roles and responsibilities of emergency services teams and SecOps teams are similar.

The Overwhelming Volume of Alerts

Over the past several years, most organizations have added new types of threat detection technologies to their networks. Each of these tools sounds an alarm when it sees anomalous or suspicious behavior. In combination, these tools create a cacophony of security alerts. SecOps analysts are simply unable to review, prioritize, and investigate all of these alerts on their own. All too often they ignore alerts, chase false positives, and make mistakes because of alert fatigue.

Research confirms the magnitude of this challenge. In its "2020 State of the SOC" report, SIEM provider Exabeam revealed that security operations centers (SOCs) are understaffed according to 39 percent of professionals who work in them — and of those, 50 percent think they need at least six additional employees. Additionally, Cisco's "2020 CISO Benchmark Study" found that organizations can investigate only 48 percent of the security alerts they receive on a given day, and of those investigated alerts, only 26 percent are deemed legitimate (Figure 4-2).

26%
Alerts Are Legitimate

50%
Legitimate Alerts Are Remediated

50%
Legitimate Alerts Are Not Remediated

48%
Alerts Are Investigated

52%
Alerts Are Not Investigated

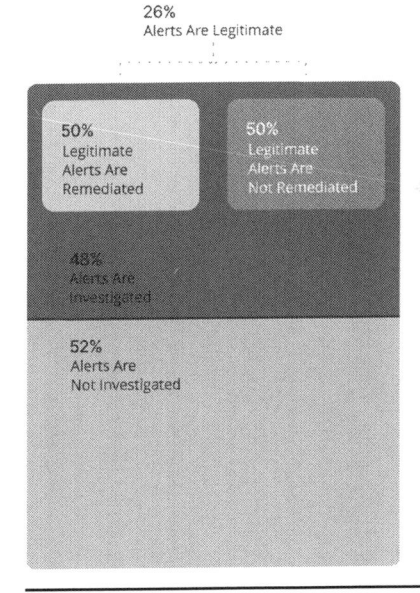

Figure 4-2: Many threat alerts are not investigated or remediated. (Source: Cisco)

Context Is King

SecOps intelligence is security intelligence that is used specifically to support triage by enriching internal alerts with the external information and context necessary to make risk-based decisions. Context is critical for rapid triage, and also very important for scoping and containing incidents.

Triage requires lots of context

A huge part of an average SecOps analyst's day is spent responding to alerts generated by internal security systems, such as SIEM or endpoint detection and response (EDR) technologies. Sources of internal data are vital in identifying potentially malicious network activity or a data breach.

Unfortunately, this data is often difficult to interpret in isolation. Determining if an alert is relevant and urgent requires gathering related information (context) from a wide variety of internal system logs, network devices, and security tools (Figure 4-3), *and* from external threat databases. Searching all of these threat data sources for context around each alert is hugely time consuming.

Key Aspects	Security Monitoring Requirement
Business Traffic Crossing a Boundary	Traffic exchanges are authorized and conform to security policy. Transport of malicious content and other forms of attack by manipulation of business traffic are detected and alerted.
Activity at a Boundary	Detect suspect activity indicative of the actions of an attacker attempting to breach the system boundary, or other deviation from normal business behavior.
Internal Workstation, Server, or Device	Detect changes to device status and configuration from accidental or deliberate acts by a user, or by malware.
Internal Network Activity	Detect suspicious activity that may indicate attacks by internal users, or external attackers who have penetrated the internal network.
Network Connections	Prevent unauthorized connections to the network made by remote access, VPN, wireless, or any other transient means of network connection.
Session Activity By User and Work Station	Detect unauthorized activity and access that is suspicious or violates security policy requirements.
Alerting on Events	Be able to respond to security incidents in a time frame appropriate to the perceived criticality of the incident.
Accurate Time in Logs	Be able to correlate event data collected from disparate sources.
Data Backup Status	Be able to recover from an event that compromises the integrity or availability of information assets.

Figure 4-3: Key aspects of security monitoring and internal sources of context. (Source: UK NCSC)

Use case: Correlating and enriching alerts

An analyst attempting to triage an initial alert without access to enough context is like a person trying to understand a news story after reading just the headline. Even when the analyst has access to external information in the form of threat feeds (Figure 4-4), that information is very hard to assimilate and correlate with other data related to the alert.

2020-09-13 02:46:26	E	63.153.27.53	offline
2020-09-12 21:41:44	E	75.130.100.165	online
2020-09-12 18:54:45	E	71.172.252.50	online
2020-09-12 15:51:16	E	118.189.9.243	offline
2020-09-12 14:11:41	E	31.167.248.50	offline
2020-09-12 08:32:01	E	78.134.74.39	online
2020-09-12 05:03:02	E	42.114.73.81	offline
2020-09-12 04:56:53	E	216.59.200.206	offline
2020-09-11 11:35:10	E	183.82.97.20	offline
2020-09-11 08:59:59	E	128.2.98.139	offline
2020-09-11 08:12:12	E	47.38.231.174	offline
2020-09-11 08:01:28	E	217.36.122.251	offline
2020-09-11 07:45:59	E	107.184.160.132	offline
2020-09-11 06:45:54	E	71.75.206.192	online
2020-09-11 06:43:49	E	123.231.21.141	offline
2020-09-11 05:54:51	E	189.222.75.8	offline
2020-09-11 05:54:51	E	189.211.177.113	offline
2020-09-11 05:54:51	E	92.27.115.15	offline
2020-09-11 05:54:51	E	207.107.101.210	offline
2020-09-11 05:31:45	E	185.97.32.6	online

Figure 4-4: It is very difficult to find relevant information in a raw threat feed and correlate it with other data related to an alert.

SecOps intelligence completely transforms this situation. It has the capability to automatically enrich threat data into intelligence and correlate it with alerts, as illustrated in Figure 4-5. The context provided might include first and most recent references to a piece of malware or a suspicious IP address, the number of sightings, associations with attack types and specific threat actors, and descriptions of the behavior of the malware or the uses of the IP address (say, as part of a botnet).

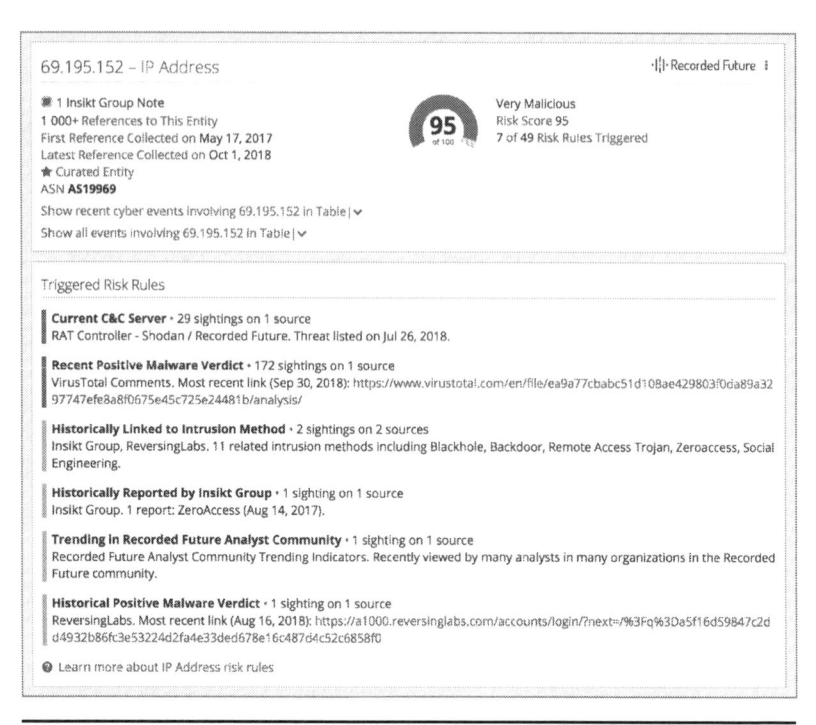

```
69.195.152 – IP Address                                              ·|¦|· Recorded Future  ⋮

✱ 1 Insikt Group Note                          ⬤      Very Malicious
1 000+ References to This Entity              ( 95 )  Risk Score 95
First Reference Collected on May 17, 2017      ⬤      7 of 49 Risk Rules Triggered
Latest Reference Collected on Oct 1, 2018     of 100
★ Curated Entity
ASN AS19969
Show recent cyber events involving 69.195.152 in Table | ⌄
Show all events involving 69.195.152 in Table | ⌄

Triggered Risk Rules

Current C&C Server • 29 sightings on 1 source
RAT Controller - Shodan / Recorded Future. Threat listed on Jul 26, 2018.

Recent Positive Malware Verdict • 172 sightings on 1 source
VirusTotal Comments. Most recent link (Sep 30, 2018): https://www.virustotal.com/en/file/ea9a77cbabc51d108ae429803f0da89a32
97747efe8a8f0675e45c725e24481b/analysis/

Historically Linked to Intrusion Method • 2 sightings on 2 sources
Insikt Group, ReversingLabs. 11 related intrusion methods including Blackhole, Backdoor, Remote Access Trojan, Zeroaccess, Social
Engineering.

Historically Reported by Insikt Group • 1 sighting on 1 source
Insikt Group. 1 report: ZeroAccess (Aug 14, 2017).

Trending in Recorded Future Analyst Community • 1 sighting on 1 source
Recorded Future Analyst Community Trending Indicators. Recently viewed by many analysts in many organizations in the Recorded
Future community.

Historical Positive Malware Verdict • 1 sighting on 1 source
ReversingLabs. Most recent link (Aug 16, 2018): https://a1000.reversinglabs.com/accounts/login/?next=/%3Fq%3Da5f16d59847c2d
d4932b86fc3e53224d2fa4e33ded678e16c487d4c52c6858f0

ⓘ Learn more about IP Address risk rules
```

Figure 4-5: A SecOps intelligence solution automatically enriches alerts with context such as previous sightings, associations with attack types and threat actors, and risk scores. (Source: Recorded Future)

This enrichment enables SecOps analysts to quickly identify the most significant threats and take immediate, informed actions to resolve them.

Enrichment empowers even relatively junior SecOps analysts to "punch above their weight" by making connections that otherwise would have required more experience than they have. It also provides a form of accelerated on-the-job training by supplying in-depth information about the latest threats.

TECH TALK

As an example of this upskilling for relatively junior analysts, suppose an alert is generated when an unknown external IP address attempts to connect over TCP port 445. Experienced analysts might know that a recent exploit for SMB has been used by ransomware to propagate itself and would identify the IP as likely to be compromised based on the owner, location, and open source data. An inexperienced analyst might not be able to make these connections unaided, but contextualized

SecOps intelligence would show the analyst that other devices on the network use SMB on port 445 to transfer files and data between servers. It would also inform the analyst that the new exploit and ransomware have been associated with that IP address.

Shortening the "Time to No"

As important as it is for SecOps analysts to gather information about real threats more quickly and accurately, there is an argument to be made that the ability to rapidly rule out false alarms is even more important.

Security intelligence provides SecOps staff with the context required to triage alerts promptly and with far less effort. It prevents analysts from wasting hours pursuing alerts based on:

- ☑ Actions that are likely to be innocuous rather than malicious
- ☑ Attacks that are not relevant to their organization
- ☑ Attacks for which defenses and controls are already in place

Some SecOps intelligence solutions automatically perform much of this filtering by customizing risk feeds to ignore or downgrade alerts that do not match organization- and industry-specific criteria.

Chapter 5

SecOps Intelligence Part 2 – Response

In this chapter

- Learn how security intelligence minimizes reactivity
- Review characteristics of security intelligence solutions that make them effective for meeting incident response challenges
- Explore incident response teams' use cases for security intelligence

"Care shouldn't start in the emergency room."

— James Douglas

After real attacks have been identified, incident response processes kick in. But both of these workflows have become more stressful for security teams. Among the reasons:

- ☑ Cyber incident volumes have increased steadily for two decades.
- ☑ Threats have become more complex and harder to analyze; staying on top of the shifting threat landscape has become a major task in itself.
- ☑ When responding to security incidents, analysts are forced to spend significant time manually checking and disseminating data from disparate sources.
- ☑ Containment of attacks and eradication of vulnerabilities continually grow more difficult.

As a result, incident response teams routinely operate under enormous time pressures and often are unable to contain cyber incidents promptly.

Continuing Challenges

While it's difficult to be precise about the number of incidents experienced by a typical organization, there is no doubt that cyberattack volume is growing rapidly. According to the Malwarebytes Labs "2020 State of Malware Report," the volume of detected attacks on businesses increased by 13 percent in 2019. While some of this growing pressure is mitigated by preventative technologies, a huge additional strain is nonetheless being placed on incident response teams because of the following factors.

The skills gap

Incident response is not an entry-level security function. It encompasses a vast swath of skills, including static and dynamic malware analysis, reverse engineering, and digital forensics. It requires analysts who have experience in the industry and are able to perform complex operations under pressure.

The highly publicized cybersecurity skills gap has grown consistently wider over the past decade. Cyber Seek calculates that there are currently more than half a million cybersecurity job openings in the United States alone. According to the ISSA-ESG report "The Life and Times of Cybersecurity Professionals 2020," 70 percent of organizations are negatively impacted by the shortage of cybersecurity professionals.

Rising response times

When you have too few skilled personnel and too many alerts, there's only one outcome: The time to resolve genuine security incidents will increase. According to the "2020 Cost of a Data Breach Report" from Ponemon Institute and IBM Security, the time to detect and contain a data breach increased from 257 days in 2017 to 280 days in 2020.

Of course, cybercriminals have no such constraints. Once they gain a foothold inside a target network, the time to compromise is usually measured in minutes. We will discuss this more in the next chapter.

A piecemeal approach

Most organizations have security groups that grow organically in parallel with increases in cyber risk. As a result, many only add security technologies and processes then they must address specific needs, and they do so without a strategic design.

While this ad hoc approach is perfectly normal, it forces incident response teams to spend a lot of time aggregating data and context from a variety of security technologies (e.g., SIEM, EDR, and firewall logs) and threat feeds. This effort significantly extends response times and increases the likelihood of mistakes.

The Reactivity Problem

Once an alert is flagged, it must be triaged, remediated, and followed up as quickly as possible to minimize cyber risk. Consider a typical incident response process:

1. **Incident detection** — Receive an alert from a SIEM, EDR, or similar product.
2. **Discovery** — Determine what has happened and how to respond.
3. **Triage and containment** — Take immediate actions to mitigate the threat and minimize damage.
4. **Remediation** — Repair damage and remove infections.
5. **Push to BAU** — Pass the incident to "business as usual" teams for final actions.

Notice the reactive nature of this process. For most organizations, nearly all the work necessary to remediate an incident is back-loaded, meaning it can't be completed until after an alert is flagged. Although this is inevitable to some degree, it is far from ideal when incident response teams are already struggling to resolve incidents quickly enough.

Minimizing Reactivity in Incident Response

To reduce response times, incident response teams must become less reactive. Two areas where advanced preparation is especially impactful are identification of probable threats and prioritization.

Identification of probable threats

When an incident response team identifies the most commonly faced threats in advance, it enables them to develop strong, consistent processes to cope with them. This preparation dramatically reduces the time the team needs to contain individual incidents and prevent mistakes, and it frees up analysts to address new and unexpected threats when they arise.

Prioritization

Not all threats are equal. When incident response teams understand which threat vectors pose the greatest level of risk to their organization, they are able to allocate their time and resources accordingly.

> **ON THE WEB**
> To find out how security experts use security intelligence to reduce reactivity in incident response, watch the joint Recorded Future and LIFARS webinar "Fuel Incident Response With Security Intelligence to Lower Breach Impact."

Strengthening Incident Response With Security Intelligence

It should be clear from our discussion so far that security technologies *alone* can't do enough to reduce pressure on human analysts.

Security intelligence reduces the demands on incident response teams and addresses many of the issues we have been reviewing by:

- ☑ Automatically identifying and dismissing false positive alerts
- ☑ Enriching alerts with real-time context from across the open web and dark web
- ☑ Assembling and comparing information from internal and external data sources to identify genuine threats
- ☑ Scoring threats according to the organization's specific needs and infrastructure

In other words, security intelligence — especially SecOps intelligence — provides incident response teams with exactly the actionable insights they need to make faster, better decisions, while holding back the tide of irrelevant and unreliable alerts that typically make their job so difficult.

SecOps Intelligence in Action

Let's look at three use cases and one abuse case that show how SecOps intelligence affects incident response teams in the real world.

Use case: Prepare processes in advance

As noted earlier, typical incident response processes are highly reactive, with most activity happening only after an incident occurs. This extends the time needed to scope and remediate incidents.

SecOps intelligence empowers incident response teams to prepare for threats by providing:

- ☑ A comprehensive, up-to-date picture of the threat landscape
- ☑ Information about popular threat actor TTPs
- ☑ Highlights of industry- and region-specific attack trends

SecOps intelligence empowers incident response teams to develop and maintain strong processes for the most common incidents and threats. Having these processes available speeds up incident discovery, triage, and containment. It also greatly improves the consistency and reliability of actions across the incident response function.

Use case: Scope and contain incidents

When an incident occurs, incident response analysts must make quick determinations about three factors:

1. What happened
2. What the incident might mean for the organization
3. Which actions to take

These factors must be analyzed as quickly as possible with a high degree of accuracy. SecOps intelligence makes a measurable impact by:

- ☑ Automatically dismissing false positives, enabling teams to focus on genuine security incidents
- ☑ Enriching incidents with related information from across the open and dark web, making it easier to determine how much of a threat they pose and how the organization might be affected
- ☑ Providing details about the threat and insights about the attacker TTPs, empowering the team to make fast and effective containment and remediation decisions

---

Is Time Your Friend or Enemy?

Ever wondered how the balance of power fluctuates between attackers and defenders as time goes by? To find out, read the Recorded Future blog post "The 4th in the 5th: Temporal Aspects of Cyber Operations."

Use case: Detect data breaches sooner

It's common for organizations to take a long time to realize a breach has occurred. According to the IBM "Cost of a Data Breach Report 2020," the average time to identify a data breach is 207 days.

Not surprisingly, stolen data and proprietary assets often turn up for sale on the dark web before their rightful owners realize what's happened.

A powerful SecOps intelligence capability provides a tremendous advantage by alerting you to a breach and providing early warning that your assets are exposed online, or someone is offering those assets for sale.

Obtaining this intelligence in real time is vital because it enables you to contain the incident as quickly as possible and identify when and how your network was breached.

Abuse case: Half measures are worse than nothing

We want to caution you about one abuse case where security intelligence may actually undermine incident response.

At the start of their security intelligence journey, some organizations opt for a minimalist solution such as a SecOps intelligence solution paired with a variety of free threat feeds. They might believe that this "dip our toes in the water" approach will minimize up-front costs.

While this type of implementation arms incident response teams with some actionable intelligence, it generally makes things worse by forcing analysts to wade through vast quantities of false positives and irrelevant alerts. To fully address the primary incident response pain points, a security intelligence capability must be comprehensive, relevant, contextualized, and integrated.

Essential Characteristics of Security Intelligence for Incident Response

Now it's time to examine the characteristics of a powerful security intelligence capability, and how they address the greatest pain points for incident response teams.

Comprehensive

To be valuable to incident response teams, security intelligence must be captured automatically from the widest possible range of locations across open sources, technical feeds, and the dark web. Otherwise analysts will be forced to conduct their own manual research to ensure nothing important has been missed.

TECH TALK

Imagine that an analyst needs to know whether an IP address has been associated with malicious activity. If she is confident that her security intelligence has been drawn from a comprehensive range of threat sources, she is able to query the data instantly and be sure the result will be accurate. If she isn't confident, she will have to spend time manually checking the IP address against several threat data sources. Figure 5-1 shows how SecOps intelligence might connect an IP address with the Trickbot malware. This kind of intelligence can be correlated with internal network logs to reveal indicators of compromise.

Chapter 5: SecOps Intelligence Part 2 – Response | 43

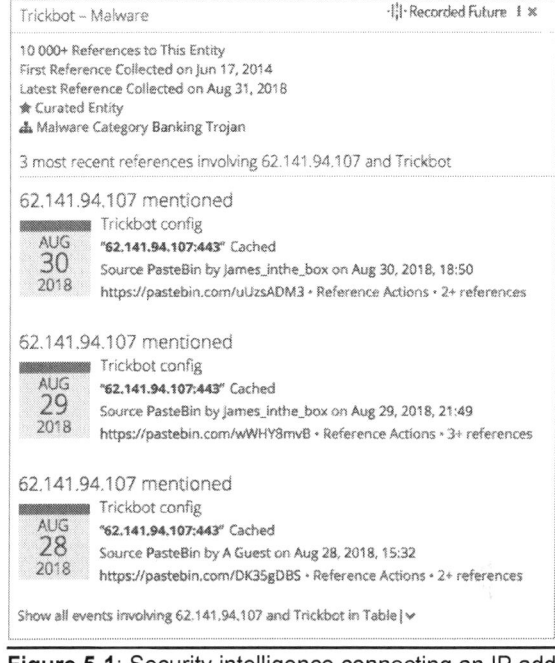

```
Trickbot – Malware                              Recorded Future

10 000+ References to This Entity
First Reference Collected on Jun 17, 2014
Latest Reference Collected on Aug 31, 2018
★ Curated Entity
♣ Malware Category Banking Trojan

3 most recent references involving 62.141.94.107 and Trickbot

62.141.94.107 mentioned
         Trickbot config
  AUG    "62.141.94.107:443" Cached
  30     Source PasteBin by James_inthe_box on Aug 30, 2018, 18:50
  2018   https://pastebin.com/uUzsADM3 • Reference Actions • 2+ references

62.141.94.107 mentioned
         Trickbot config
  AUG    "62.141.94.107:443" Cached
  29     Source PasteBin by James_inthe_box on Aug 29, 2018, 21:49
  2018   https://pastebin.com/wWHY8mvB • Reference Actions • 3+ references

62.141.94.107 mentioned
         Trickbot config
  AUG    "62.141.94.107:443" Cached
  28     Source PasteBin by A Guest on Aug 28, 2018, 15:32
  2018   https://pastebin.com/DK35gDBS • Reference Actions • 2+ references

Show all events involving 62.141.94.107 and Trickbot in Table | ˅
```

Figure 5-1: Security intelligence connecting an IP address with the Trickbot malware. (Source: Recorded Future)

ON THE WEB

For a discussion of how to distill massive quantities of data to produce a small but steady stream of actionable security intelligence, read the Recorded Future blog post, "Security Intelligence, Information, and Data: What Is the Difference?"

Relevant

It's impossible to avoid all false positives when working to identify and contain incidents. But SecOps intelligence empowers incident response teams to quickly identify and purge false positives generated by security technologies such as SIEM and EDR products.

There are two categories of false positives to consider:

1. Alerts that are relevant to an organization but are inaccurate or unhelpful
2. Alerts that are accurate and/or interesting but aren't relevant to the organization

Both types have the potential to waste an enormous amount of an incident response analyst's time.

Advanced security intelligence products are now employing powerful algorithms and analytical processes to identify and discard false positives automatically and draw analysts' attention to the most important (i.e., most relevant) intelligence.

> **CAUTION:** If you don't choose your security intelligence technology carefully, your team is likely to waste a great deal of time on intelligence that's inaccurate, outdated, or irrelevant to your organization.

Contextualized

Not all threats are created equal. Even among relevant threat alerts, some will inevitably be more urgent and important than the rest. An alert from a single source could be both accurate and relevant, but still not particularly high in priority. That is why context is so important: It provides critical clues about which alerts will most likely matter to your organization.

Contextual intelligence related to an alert might include:

- ☑ Corroboration from multiple sources that the same type of alert has been associated with recent attacks
- ☑ Confirmation that it has been associated with threat actors known to be active in your industry
- ☑ A timeline showing that the alert occurred slightly before or after other events linked with attacks

Modern analytics and algorithms make it possible for a security intelligence solution to consider multiple sources concurrently and determine which alerts are most important to a specific organization.

Integrated

Among the most critical characteristics of a security intelligence product is its ability to integrate with a broad range of security tools, including SIEM and incident response solutions. Through integration, the product is able to examine the alerts they generate and:

- ☑ Determine whether each alert should be dismissed as a false positive
- ☑ Score the alert according to its importance
- ☑ Enrich the alert with valuable extra context

Effective integration eliminates the need for analysts to manually compare each alert to information found across their ecosystem of security and security intelligence tools. Even more important, integration and automated processes are able to filter out a huge number of false positives without any checking by a human analyst. Saving time and avoiding frustration are perhaps security intelligence's greatest benefits for incident response teams.

Chapter 6

Vulnerability Intelligence

In this chapter

- Examine the current challenges to addressing vulnerabilities based on actual risk
- Learn how vulnerability intelligence delivers insights into threat actor behaviors
- See how risk-based intelligence streamlines the operational elements of vulnerability management

"The acknowledgment of our weakness is the first step in repairing our loss."

— Thomas à Kempis

Vulnerability management is not glamorous, but it is one of the very few ways to be proactive in securing your organization. Its importance cannot be overstated.

The key to success in vulnerability management is to shift the thinking of your security teams from trying to patch everything to making risk-based decisions. That is critical because the vast ocean of vulnerabilities disclosed each year puts incredible stress on the teams responsible for identifying vulnerable assets and deploying patches. To make smart risk-based decisions, take advantage of more sources of security intelligence.

The Vulnerability Problem by the Numbers

According to the Gartner Market Guide for Security Threat Intelligence Products and Services, about 8,000 vulnerabilities a year were disclosed over the past decade. The number increased only slightly from year to year, and only about one in eight of those vulnerabilities were actually exploited. However, during the same period, the amount of new software coming into use grew immensely, and the number of threats has increased exponentially.

In other words, although the number of breaches and threats has increased over the past 10 years, only a small percentage were based on new vulnerabilities. As Gartner puts it, "More threats are leveraging the same small set of vulnerabilities."

Zero day does not mean top priority

Zero-day threats regularly draw an outsized amount of attention. However, the vast majority of new threats labeled as zero days are actually variations on a theme, exploiting the same old vulnerabilities in slightly different ways. The implication is that the most effective approach to vulnerability management is not to focus on zero-day threats, but rather to identify and patch the vulnerabilities in the software your organization uses.

Time is of the essence

Threat actors have gotten quicker at exploiting vulnerabilities. According to Gartner, the average time it takes between the identification of a vulnerability and the appearance of an exploit in the wild has dropped from 45 days to 15 days over the last decade.

This trend has two implications for vulnerability management teams:

1. You have roughly two weeks to patch or remediate your systems against a new exploit.
2. If you can't patch in that timeframe, you need a plan to mitigate the damage.

Research from IBM X-Force shows that if a vulnerability is not exploited within two weeks to three months after it is announced, it is statistically unlikely that it ever will be exploited. Therefore "old" vulnerabilities are usually not a priority for patching.

ON THE WEB

For insights on recent vulnerabilities, read the Recorded Future threat analysis of "The Top 10 Vulnerabilities Used by Cybercriminals in 2019." Exploits usually target the most widely used technologies. An episode of the Recorded Future podcast entitled "7 of the Top 10 Vulnerabilities Target Microsoft" explains why.

DON'T FORGET

All of these statistics point to one conclusion: Your goal should not be to patch the most vulnerabilities, or even the most zero-day threats, but rather to identify and address the vulnerabilities most likely to be exploited against your organization.

Assess Risk Based on Exploitability

Consider this comparison: If patching vulnerabilities to keep your network safe is like getting vaccines to protect yourself from disease, then you need to identify which vaccinations are priorities and which are unnecessary. You may need a flu shot every season to stay healthy, but there's no need to stay vaccinated against yellow fever or malaria unless you will be exposed to them.

Two of the greatest values of a vulnerability intelligence solution are identification of specific vulnerabilities that represent actual risk to your organization and visibility into their likelihood of exploitation.

Figure 6-1 illustrates the point. Thousands of vulnerabilities have been disclosed. Hundreds are being exploited, and some number of vulnerabilities exist in your environment. You really only need to be concerned about the ones that lie within the intersection of those last two categories — vulnerabilities that are in your environment and are actively being exploited.

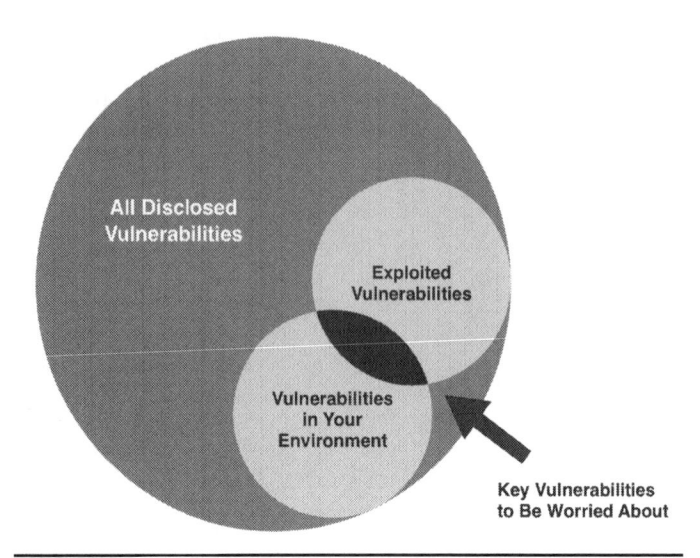

Figure 6-1: The greatest actual risks are vulnerabilities that are present in your organization's environment and are currently being exploited. (Source: Gartner)

Severity ratings are often misleading

Ranking threats in terms of severity is a mistake that vulnerability managers make regularly. Classification and ranking systems like Common Vulnerabilities and Exposures (CVE) naming and the Common Vulnerability Scoring System (CVSS) don't take into account whether threat actors are actually exploiting vulnerabilities right now in your industry or locations. Relying solely on vulnerability severity is often like getting a vaccine for the bubonic plague instead of a flu shot because the plague killed more people at some point in history.

The Genesis of Security Intelligence: Vulnerability Databases

Vulnerability databases consolidate information on disclosed vulnerabilities and also score their exploitability.

In fact, one of the very first forms of security intelligence was NIST's National Vulnerability Database (NVD). It centralizes information on disclosed vulnerabilities to make it easier for organizations to see if they were likely to be affected. For more than 20 years, the NVD has collected information on almost 150,000 vulnerabilities, making it an invaluable source for information security professionals. Nations including China and Russia have followed NIST's lead by setting up vulnerability databases.

ON THE WEB Find the NIST NVD at https://nvd.nist.gov/. A catalog of vulnerability databases is published by the industry organization FIRST here: https://www.first.org/global/sigs/vrdx/vdb-catalog.

CAUTION There are two significant limitations to most vulnerability databases:

1. They focus on technical exploitability rather than active exploitation.
2. They are not updated fast enough to provide warning of some quickly spreading threats.

Exploitability versus exploitation

Information in vulnerability databases is almost entirely focused on technical exploitability – a judgment of how likely it is that exploiting a particular vulnerability will result in greater or lesser damage to systems and networks. In the NVD, this is measured through the CVSS scoring system.

Technical exploitability and active exploitation are not the same thing, though. CVSS base scores provide a metric that's reasonably accurate and easy to understand, but you need to know what information the score is conveying. Unless a base score is modified by a temporal score or an environmental score (https://www.first.org/cvss/calculator/3.0), it really only tells you how bad the vulnerability is hypothetically, not whether it's actually being exploited in the wild.

Figure 6-2 shows the kind of security intelligence that a vulnerability intelligence tool provides. In this case, the risk a vulnerability poses is determined based on reports involving the CVE's appearance before it has been assigned a CVSS score by NVD.

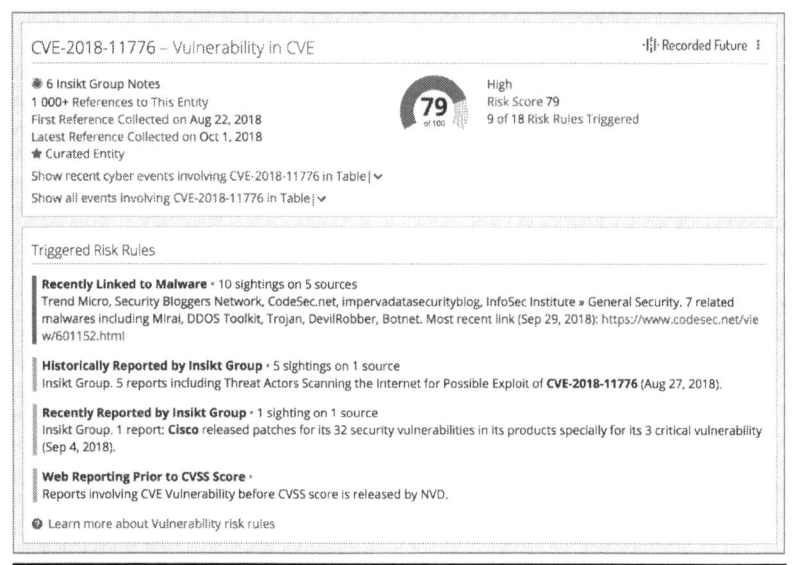

```
CVE-2018-11776 -- Vulnerability in CVE                                    Recorded Future

  6 Insikt Group Notes                              High
  1 000+ References to This Entity           79    Risk Score 79
  First Reference Collected on Aug 22, 2018  of 100 9 of 18 Risk Rules Triggered
  Latest Reference Collected on Oct 1, 2018
  ★ Curated Entity
  Show recent cyber events involving CVE-2018-11776 in Table ⌄
  Show all events involving CVE-2018-11776 in Table ⌄

Triggered Risk Rules

  Recently Linked to Malware • 10 sightings on 5 sources
  Trend Micro, Security Bloggers Network, CodeSec.net, impervadatasecurityblog, InfoSec Institute » General Security. 7 related
  malwares including Mirai, DDOS Toolkit, Trojan, DevilRobber, Botnet. Most recent link (Sep 29, 2018): https://www.codesec.net/vie
  w/601152.html

  Historically Reported by Insikt Group • 5 sightings on 1 source
  Insikt Group. 5 reports including Threat Actors Scanning the Internet for Possible Exploit of CVE-2018-11776 (Aug 27, 2018).

  Recently Reported by Insikt Group • 1 sighting on 1 source
  Insikt Group. 1 report: Cisco released patches for its 32 security vulnerabilities in its products specially for its 3 critical vulnerability
  (Sep 4, 2018).

  Web Reporting Prior to CVSS Score •
  Reports involving CVE Vulnerability before CVSS score is released by NVD.

  ⓘ Learn more about Vulnerability risk rules
```

Figure 6-2: Security intelligence related to a vulnerability. (Source: Recorded Future)

TECH TALK

An object lesson in the difference between the NVD's "official risk" and "real risk" from a vulnerability in the wild is CVE-2017-0022. Despite having a CVSS severity score of only 4.3 (in the medium range), Recorded Future considered it one of the top 10 vulnerabilities in use in 2017. The real risk was very high because threat actors added this vulnerability to the widespread Neutrino Exploit Kit, where it performed a critical role checking whether security software is installed on a target system.

Chapter 6: Vulnerability Intelligence | 53

Next week versus now

Lack of timeliness is another shortcoming of many vulnerability databases. For example, an analysis by Recorded Future found that 75 percent of disclosed vulnerabilities appear on other online sources before they appear in the NVD — and on average it takes those vulnerabilities a week to show up there. This is a very serious problem, because it handicaps security teams in the race to patch a vulnerability before adversaries are able to exploit it, as illustrated in Figure 6-3.

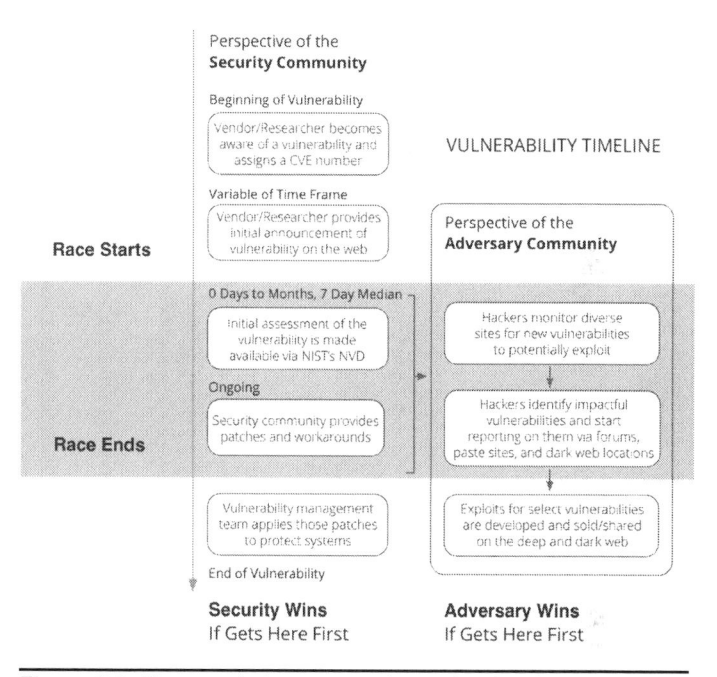

Figure 6-3: The race between security professionals and adversaries.

TECH TALK

The informal way in which vulnerabilities are disclosed and announced contributes to the delay in recognizing them in vulnerability databases. Typically, a vendor or researcher discloses the vulnerability to the NVD, which assigns a CVE number and begins an analysis. In the meantime, the vendor or researcher publishes more information on its own blog or a social media account. Good luck collating data from these disparate and hard-to-find sources before threat actors develop proof-of-concept malware and add it to exploit kits!

> **ON THE WEB** For details on the processes that threat actors use to exploit vulnerabilities, see the Recorded Future blog post "Behind the Scenes of the Adversary Exploit Process."

Vulnerability Intelligence and Real Risk

The most effective way to assess the true risk of a vulnerability to your organization is to combine all of the following:

- ☑ Internal vulnerability scanning data
- ☑ External intelligence from a wide variety of sources
- ☑ An understanding of why threat actors are targeting certain vulnerabilities and ignoring others

Internal vulnerability scanning

Almost every vulnerability management team scans internal systems for vulnerabilities, correlates the results with information reported in vulnerability databases, and uses the correlation to determine what to patch. This is a basic use of operational security intelligence, even if we don't usually think of it that way.

Conventional scanning is an excellent way to deprioritize vulnerabilities that don't appear on your systems. By itself, however, scanning is not an adequate way to accurately prioritize vulnerabilities that are found.

Risk milestones for vulnerabilities

One powerful way to assess a vulnerability's risk is to look at how far it has progressed from initial identification to availability, weaponization, and commoditization in exploit kits.

The level of real risk increases dramatically as the vulnerability passes through the milestones shown in Figure 6-4. Broad-based vulnerability intelligence reveals a vulnerability's progress along this path.

External Factors

Level of Risk

1. Identified | 2. Disclosed | 3. Published Proof of Concept | 4. Scanner Availability | 5. Weaponized in Malcode | 6. Commoditized in Exploit Kits

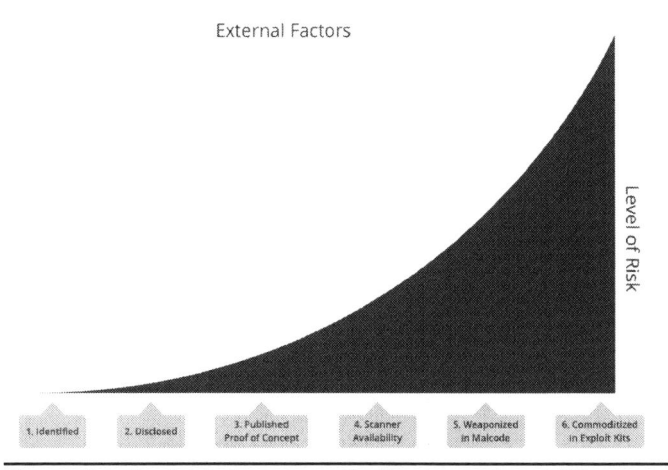

Figure 6-4: Real risk rises dramatically when vulnerabilities become weaponized and commoditized.

Understanding the adversary

As discussed elsewhere in this book, good security intelligence should not simply provide information in the form of scores and statistics. That's why vulnerability intelligence leads to a deeper understanding of how and why threat actors are targeting certain vulnerabilities and ignoring others. Below we discuss sources of intelligence that contribute to this understanding.

How to Create Meaningful Risk Scores

Beyond technical characteristics, what are the factors that can be used to calculate risk scores of vulnerabilities? Recorded Future's native risk scoring system incorporates data about criminal adoption, patterns in exploit sharing, and the number of links to malware. This information often comes from sources that are difficult to access, like forums on the dark web.

Sources of Intelligence

Data from asset scans and external vulnerability databases are only the starting points for generating intelligence that enables you to assess the risk of vulnerabilities. Unless vulnerability intelligence includes data from a wide range and variety of sources, analysts risk missing emerging vulnerabilities until it's too late.

Valuable sources of information for assessing true risk to your business include:

- ☑ **Information security sites** like vendor blogs, official disclosure information on vulnerabilities, and security news sites
- ☑ **Social media**, where link sharing provides jumping-off points for uncovering useful intelligence
- ☑ **Code repositories** such as GitHub, which yield insights into the development of proof-of-concept code for exploiting vulnerabilities
- ☑ **Paste sites** such as Pastebin and Ghostbin (which are sometimes wrongly defined as dark web sources) that often house lists of exploitable vulnerabilities
- ☑ **The dark web**, composed of communities and marketplaces with a barrier to entry, where exploits are developed, shared, and sold
- ☑ **Forums** with no barrier to entry or requirement to be using specific software, where threat actors exchange information on vulnerabilities and exploits
- ☑ **Technical feeds** that deliver data streams of potentially malicious indicators, which add useful context around the activities of malware and exploit kits

Vulnerability Chatter on the Dark Web

There are several reasons why it's difficult (and potentially dangerous) to eavesdrop on the channels that threat actors use to communicate and operate:

- Underground forums are hard to find (after all, there's no Google for the dark web).

- Threat actors change locations whenever they feel their anonymity is at risk.

- It takes a lot of searching to find the crumbs of information that are relevant to your security.

- Access may require entrance fees or endorsements from existing members of the community.

- Many of these forums operate exclusively in local languages (Figure 6-5).

Security intelligence vendors with expertise in collecting and analyzing dark web intelligence come into play here. They offer contextualized information from dark web forums on vulnerabilities directly relevant to your network, without putting you or your organization in harm's way.

PDF CVE-2018-4990 и CVE-2018-8120

Posted in Dark Web Forum
Posts in thread 15
First posting Jun 28 2018, 04:02
Most recent posting Aug 07 2020, 23:31

Translated from Russian:
Electronic Document **Exploitation Kit** The kit consists of several groups of exploits separated by targeting and a place in the exploit chain. Since **Adobe** Reader, starting with **Aobe Reader** X, uses a sandbox to isolate the process, at least 2 exploits are required to successfully exploit **Adobe** Reader and then exit the sandbox. This package includes exploits for the following vulnerabilities in **Acrobat Reader** : **CVE-2018-4985** - code execution in the **Adobe** Reader (Out of bounds) sandbox **CVE-2018-4990** - code execution in the **Adobe** Reader (Double free) sandbox **CVE-2018-4901** - code execution in the **Adobe** Reader sandbox (**Use after free**) **CVE-2018-4872** - sandbox bypassing **Adobe** Reader (logical bug) **CVE-2018-4993** - disclosing the NTLM hash (logical bug) **CVE-2018-12815** -
Show original

Post 11 of 15 by Ondrik8 on Jul 12 2018, 16:48

Translated from Russian:
Quote (**Ondrik8 @ 12.07.2018, 22:48**) **Electronic** Document Exploitation Kit The kit includes several groups exploit separated by Target and the place to exploit the chain. Since **Adobe** Reader, starting with **Aobe Reader** X, uses a sandbox to isolate the process, at least 2 exploits are required to successfully exploit **Adobe** Reader and then exit the sandbox. This package includes exploits for the following wing vulnerabilities in **Acrobat Reader** : **CVE-2018-4985** - code execution in the **Adobe** Reader (Out of bounds) sandbox **CVE-2018-4990** - code execution in the **Adobe** Reader (Double free) sandbox **CVE-2018-4901** - code execution in the **Adobe** Reader sandbox (**Use after free**) **CVE-2018-4872** - bypassing the **Adobe** Reader sandbox (logical bug)
Show original

Post 12 of 15 by OG-Zer0day on Jul 12 2018, 20:50

Figure 6-5: An exchange of information between threat actors on a dark web forum translated from Russian. (Source: Recorded Future)

Use Cases for Cross-Referencing Intelligence

To accurately assess real risk, you must be able to correlate information from multiple sources. Once you begin to understand how individual references combine to tell the whole story, you will be able to map the intelligence you have to the risk milestones a vulnerability typically goes through.

For example, you might notice a new vulnerability disclosed on a vendor's website. Then, you discover a tweet with a link to proof-of-concept exploit code on GitHub. Later, you find the code is being sold on a dark web forum. Eventually, you might see news reports of the vulnerability being exploited in the wild.

Here's another example. The website of an Information Sharing and Analysis Center (ISAC) for your industry shows that an organization like yours has been victimized by an exploit kit that attacks a vulnerability in a specialized, industry-specific software application. You find that there are four copies of that software in corners of your organization that have not been patched in three years.

TIP Cross-referencing this kind of intelligence enables you to move away from a "race to patch everything" mode of operation, and empowers you to focus on the vulnerabilities that present the greatest actual risk.

Bridging the Risk Gaps Among Security, Operations, and Business Leadership

In most organizations, the responsibility for protecting against vulnerabilities falls on the shoulders of two teams:

1. The vulnerability management team runs scans and prioritizes vulnerabilities based on potential risk.
2. The IT operations team deploys patches and remediates the affected systems.

This dynamic creates a tendency to approach vulnerability management "by the numbers." For example, the vulnerability management team in the security organization might determine that several vulnerabilities in Apache web servers pose a very high risk to the business and should be given top priority. However, the IT operations team may be supporting a lot more Windows systems than Apache servers. If team members are measured strictly on the number of systems patched, they have an incentive to keep their focus on lower-priority Windows vulnerabilities.

Intelligence on exploitability also prepares your organization to strike the correct balance between patching vulnerable systems and interrupting business operations. Most organizations have a strong aversion to disturbing business continuity. However, if you know that a patch will protect the organization against a real, imminent risk, then a short interruption is completely justified.

The risk milestones framework outlined in Figure 6-4 makes it much easier to communicate the danger of a vulnerability across your security and operations teams, up through senior managers, and even to the board of directors. This level of visibility into the rationale behind decisions made around vulnerabilities will increase confidence in the security team across your entire organization.

TIP: To reduce the gap between the vulnerability management and IT operations teams, introduce risk of exploitability as a key driver for prioritizing patches. Arming the vulnerability management team with more contextualized data about the risk of exploitability will enable them to pinpoint a smaller number of high-risk CVEs, which will result in them making fewer demands on the operations team. The operations team will then be able to give top priority to that small number of critical patches, and still have time to address their other goals.

Chapter 7

Threat Intelligence Part 1 – Knowing Attackers

In this chapter

- Explore the role of threat analysts
- See how conversations in underground communities present opportunities to gather valuable security intelligence
- Examine use cases for applying knowledge about attackers to security activities

"The challenge for capitalism is that the things that breed trust also breed the environment for fraud."

– James Surowiecki

Threat Intelligence as Part of Security Intelligence

Until recently, many of the topics discussed in this handbook were known throughout the security community as "threat intelligence." However, because the term threat intelligence has become so closely associated with information about direct threats to traditional IT systems, informed experts now use "security intelligence" to include that information, plus additional details about risks related to areas such as third parties, brand presence on websites and social media platforms outside of the corporate network, risks to physical assets around the globe, and more.

This shift has not eliminated the need for threat intelligence. It is still essential to enable threat analysts to perform their most important functions, including:

- ☑ Identifying the actors who most actively threaten the organization
- ☑ Understanding attackers' motives and targets
- ☑ Investigating and documenting their TTPs
- ☑ Tracking macro trends that affect the organization, including trends relevant to its industry and the regions where it operates.

A security intelligence solution is essential to the success of threat analysts, because it pinpoints the most relevant threats, slashes the time they spend researching them, and generates more intelligence about them — often from sources that would be difficult or impossible for analysts to find and access on their own.

In this chapter and the next we will examine several of the main responsibilities of threat analysts.

Understand Your Enemy

Threat analysts cannot focus solely on detecting and responding to threats already present in their environment. They need to anticipate attacks by gathering security intelligence about the cybercriminal gangs, state-sponsored hacking groups, ideological "hacktivists," and others who target their organizations.

As an example, let's look at the kind of intelligence you might be able to find about profit-motivated cybercriminal gangs. They are an important intelligence target, because the "Verizon 2020 Data Breach Investigations Report" attributes 55 percent of confirmed breaches to organized crime (Figure 7-1).

Who Is Behind the Breaches?

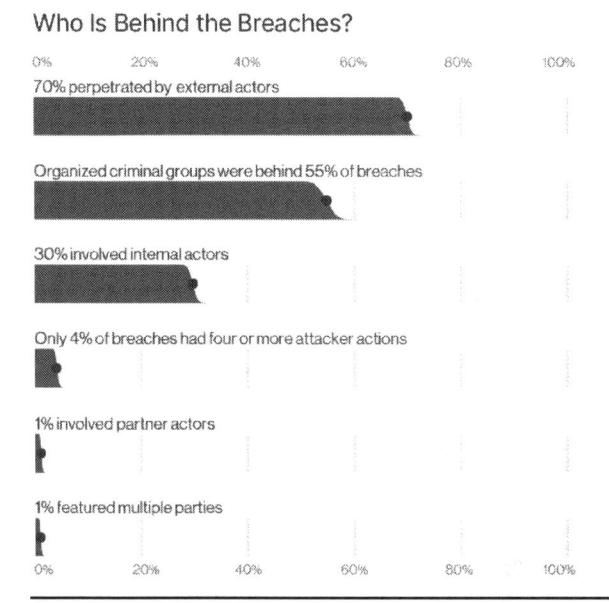

- 70% perpetrated by external actors
- Organized criminal groups were behind 55% of breaches
- 30% involved internal actors
- Only 4% of breaches had four or more attacker actions
- 1% involved partner actors
- 1% featured multiple parties

Figure 7-1: Top external actor varieties in data breaches. (Source: Verizon Data Breach Investigation Report 2020)

Intelligence gathered by Recorded Future from dark web communities shows that organized criminal groups (OCGs) are employing freelance hackers to defraud businesses and individuals. These groups operate just like legitimate businesses in many ways, with a hierarchy of members functioning as a team to create, operate, and maintain fraud schemes.

A typical OCG is controlled by a single mastermind (Figure 7-2). It might include specialists with relevant expertise for the crimes they commit. For example, bankers with extensive connections in the financial industry may arrange money laundering, forgers might be responsible for fake documents and supporting paperwork, professional project managers could oversee the technical aspects of operations, software engineers would write code, and other skilled hackers may be involved for specific tasks. Some groups even include ex-law enforcement agents who gather information and run counter-intelligence operations.

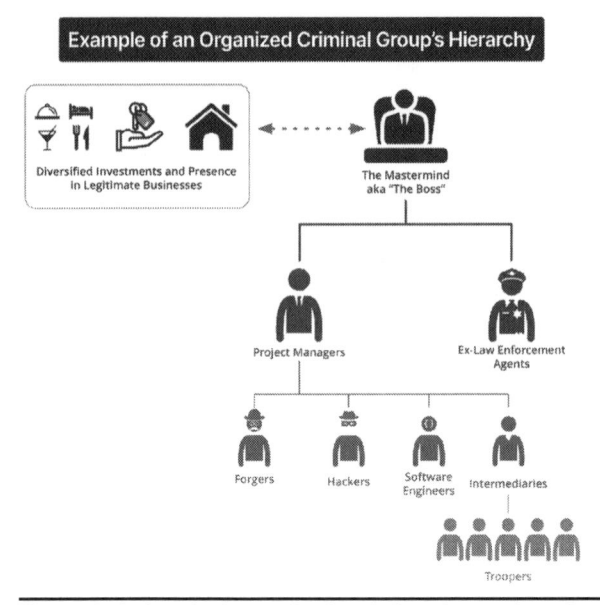

Example of an Organized Criminal Group's Hierarchy

Figure 7-2: A typical organizational chart for a cybercrime syndicate. (Source: Recorded Future)

The members of cybercrime syndicates tend to have strong ties in real life, and often are respected members of their social groups. They certainly don't regard themselves as ordinary street criminals. They rarely cross paths with what most people think of as traditional gangsters, preferring to remain in the shadows and avoid attention from law enforcement and local mafia branches. However, schemes that require large numbers of people, such as those that involve taking cash out of multiple automated teller machines simultaneously, may involve a chain of intermediaries who recruit and manage the troopers who do the leg work.

Criminal Communities and the Dark Web

Only rarely are threat analysts able to attribute a cyberattack to a single individual operating in isolation. Advanced attacks typically require a wide range of skills and tools, and an infrastructure capable of launching and supporting campaigns that use ransomware, phishing, and other technical tools and social engineering techniques.

Today, all those products and services are available for purchase or for rent in a sophisticated underground criminal economy. Cybercriminals, hackers, and their accomplices exchange information and carry out transactions related to illicit activities on the deep web (areas of the web that are not indexed by search engines) and the dark web (areas of the web that are only accessible with special software and tools that mask the identity of visitors).

Gated communities

Not all threat actors operate exclusively in what would technically be referred to as the dark web. Some build communities based on fairly standard discussion boards that are encrypted behind a login and use web collaboration technologies like Jabber and Telegram to conduct their business.

Prospective members of these underground networks are vetted by active participants in the chat rooms and forums before they are allowed to join. They may have to pay an entrance fee, ranging from US$50 to $2,000 or more. In fact, at least one forum is known to require a deposit of more than $100,000 from prospective members.

A strength — and a weakness

The dark web and criminal communities give threat actors access to information, tools, infrastructure, and contract services that multiply their power and reach. However, these communities also create risks for threat actors, because they are susceptible to monitoring — which provides security intelligence that enables security teams to anticipate and defeat attacks.

> **Know Your Dark Networks**
>
> We found that the dark web is organized in three distinct communities: low-tier underground forums, higher-tier dark web forums, and dark web markets. Analysis revealed that a significant group of actors are posting in both low-tier and higher tier forums, showing a connection between these two communities. However, dark web markets are largely disconnected from these forums. Gain a deeper understanding of how the criminal underground maintains a hierarchy of users by reading this research from Recorded Future: "Dark Networks: Social Network Analysis of Dark Web Communities."

Connecting the Dots

Security intelligence gathered from underground communities is a window into the motivations, methods, and tactics of threat actors, especially when this intelligence is correlated with information from the surface web, including technical feeds and indicators.

The power of truly contextualized security intelligence is demonstrated by its ability to draw together data from a wide variety of sources and make connections between disparate pieces of information.

For example, the following contextual information might be used to turn news about a new malware variant into security intelligence:

- ☑ Evidence that threat actors are using this malware in the wild
- ☑ Reports that exploit kits using the malware are available for sale on the dark web
- ☑ Confirmation that vulnerabilities targeted by the exploit kits are present in your organization

TIP Monitor the dark web and underground communities for direct mentions of your organization and assets. These mentions often indicate targeting or potential breaches. It's also important to monitor for mentions of your industry and other less specific terms that might point to your operations. Using security intelligence to assess risk in this way will give you greater confidence about your defenses and empower you to make better decisions.

Use Case: More Comprehensive Incident Response

When indicators of a threat are detected, SecOps teams take immediate steps to protect the targeted assets. However, they rely on threat analysts to research the attack and provide additional information to more fully shut down the attack, remediate its effects, and prevent future occurrences.

For example, threat analysts are often able to attribute an attack to a particular cybercriminal or state-sponsored hacking group and research the group's TTPs. Security teams might then use that intelligence to take steps like finding other instances of malware and phishing emails used in the attack, cleaning up affected systems, quarantining the emails, forcing password changes for compromised accounts, and taking other steps to disrupt the attacker's kill chain.

DON'T FORGET

Research for thorough incident response and remediation takes a significant amount of time. To achieve rapid response, it is critical to use a security intelligence solution with automation and integration to collect and process large volumes of data from many sources and find relevant context and insights. The security intelligence solution must also be able to automate workflows for analyzing the intelligence and disseminating it quickly to the right security teams and management, within their existing security tools and in their preferred formats.

Use Case: Proactive Threat Hunting

Most security programs are reactive, meaning they rely on alerts before taking action. However, many organizations are creating threat hunting teams to look proactively for indicators of threats before an alert is generated and ideally before the attack has progressed very far.

There are hundreds of clues that threat hunters may search for on networks and endpoints. These include: Malware files, suspicious changes to registry keys, system configurations and application permissions, unusual DLLs, scripts and drivers, misuse of utilities like PowerShell and PSExec, anomalous behaviors by JOB files, binaries that initiate connections outside of the corporate network, unusual sequences of events (such as applications that download and execute scripts on start-up), and techniques used to steal credentials.

Security intelligence solutions provide threat intelligence on the threat actors currently attacking similar organizations and the techniques and tools they use. This information enables threat hunters to avoid "boiling the ocean" by trying to capture and analyze vast amounts of data. Instead, they are able to prioritize searches for the most dangerous threats to their organization and focus on finding specific indicators and artifacts related to those attacks.

Use Case: Advance Warning of Payment Fraud

Since the birth of commerce, criminals have looked for ways to use available technology to make an easy profit from those in possession of assets. In 17th century England, for example, the growth in coach travel among an affluent merchant class, combined with the invention of the portable flintlock pistol, gave rise to the highwayman.

In our digital age, companies that conduct business and transact online find their data targeted by various forms of cyber fraud, including payment fraud.

The term "payment fraud" encompasses a wide variety of techniques by which cybercriminals profit from compromised payment data. For example, they may use phishing to collect payment card details. More-complex attacks might compromise ecommerce sites or point-of-sale systems to achieve the same goal. Once they have acquired card data, the criminals resell it (often as packs of numbers) and walk away with their cut.

One example of the effective use of threat intelligence is providing threat analysts with advance warning of upcoming attacks related to payment fraud. Monitoring sources like underground communities, paste sites, and other forums for relevant payment card numbers, bank identifier numbers, or references specific to financial institutions potentially provides visibility into nefarious operations that might affect their organization. Then the analysts can work with other security teams to forestall the planned attacks by remediating relevant vulnerabilities, increasing monitoring of targeted systems, and tightening security controls.

Chapter 8

Threat Intelligence Part 2 – Risk Analysis

In this chapter

- Explore the value of risk models like the FAIR framework
- Discover right and wrong ways to gather data about risk
- Learn how security intelligence enables you to forecast attack probabilities and the financial costs of attacks

"Establish and promote information risk management best practices that ...[achieve] the right balance between protecting the organization and running the business."

— Mission statement of the FAIR Institute

A key function of threat analysts is to model risks and empower managers to make informed decisions about reducing risk. Risk modeling offers a way to objectively assess current risks, and to estimate clear and quantifiable financial returns from investments in cybersecurity.

However, many cyber risk models suffer from either:

- ☑ Vague, non-quantified output, often in the form of "stoplight charts" that show green, yellow, and red threat levels
- ☑ Estimates about threat probabilities and costs that are hastily compiled, based on partial information, and riddled with unfounded assumptions

Non-quantified output is not very actionable, while models based on faulty input result in "garbage in, garbage out" scenarios with outputs that appear to be precise, but are actually misleading. To avoid these problems, organizations need a well-designed risk model and plenty of valid, current information — including security intelligence.

TIP Cybersecurity risk assessments should not be based only on criteria defined to prove compliance with regulations. With those criteria, assessing risk usually becomes an exercise in checking boxes against cybersecurity controls like firewalls and encryption. Counting the number of boxes checked results in a very misleading picture of actual risk.

The FAIR Risk Model

The equation at the core of any risk model is simple:

"Likelihood of occurrence times impact equals expected cost"

But, clearly, the devil is in the details. Fortunately, some very smart people have developed effective risk models and methodologies that you can use and adapt to your own needs. One that we like is the Factor Analysis of Information Risk (FAIR) model from the FAIR Institute. Figure 8-1 shows the framework of this model.

The FAIR framework is useful for creating a quantitative risk assessment model that contains specific probabilities for loss from specific kinds of threats.

ON THE WEB Learn more about FAIR at the FAIR Institute website. This quantitative model for information security and operational risk is focused on understanding, analyzing, and quantifying information risk in real financial terms.

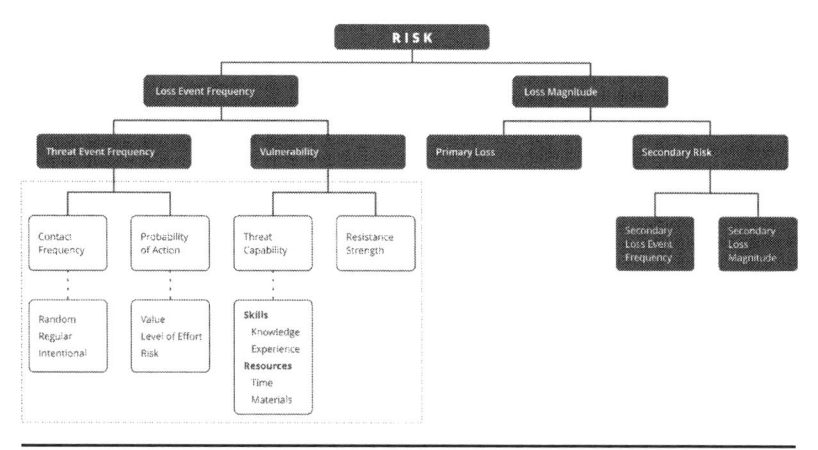

Chapter 8: Threat Intelligence Part 2 – Risk Analysis | 73

Figure 8-1: The FAIR Framework, with elements informed by intelligence highlighted. (Source: The FAIR Institute)

Measurements and transparency are key

The FAIR framework (and others like it) enable you to create risk models that:

- ☑ Make defined measurements of risk
- ☑ Are transparent about assumptions, variables, and outcomes
- ☑ Show specific loss probabilities in financial terms

Measurements, formulas, assumptions, variables, and outcomes need to be made transparent in order to be discussed, defended, and changed. Because much of the FAIR model is defined in business and financial terms, executives, line of business managers, and other stakeholders can learn to speak the same language to classify assets, threats, and vulnerabilities in the same way.

> **TIP**
> Whenever possible, incorporate specific probabilities about future losses in your risk model. Specific probabilities enable risk managers and senior executives to discuss the model and potential ways to improve it, after which their confidence in the model and the recommendations that come out of it will increase.

> **Which Statement Is More Useful?**
>
> "The threat from DDoS attacks to our business has been changed from high to medium (red to yellow)."
>
> **Or**
>
> "There is a 20 percent probability that our business will incur a loss of more than $300,000 in the next 12 months because a distributed denial-of-service (DDoS) attack will disrupt the availability of our customer-facing websites."

Security Intelligence and Threat Probabilities

As shown in the left side of Figure 8-1, a major part of creating a threat model involves estimating the probability of successful attacks (or "loss event frequency" in the language of the FAIR framework).

The first step is to create a list of threat categories that might affect the business. This list typically includes malware, phishing attacks, exploit kits, zero-day attacks, web application exploits, DDoS attacks, ransomware, and many other threats.

The next step is much more difficult: To estimate probabilities that the attacks will happen, and that they will succeed (i.e., the odds that the organization contains vulnerabilities related to the attacks and existing controls are not sufficient to stop them).

CAUTION: Avoid the following scenario: A GRC (governance, risk, and compliance) team member asks a security analyst, "What is the likelihood of our facing this particular attack?" The security analyst (who really can't win) thinks for 30 seconds about past experience and current security controls and makes a wild guess: "I dunno, maybe 20 percent."

Chapter 8: Threat Intelligence Part 2 – Risk Analysis | 75

To avoid appearing clueless, your security team needs answers that are better informed than that. Security intelligence, and specifically threat intelligence, makes it possible to answer questions such as:

- ☑ Which threat actors are using this attack, and do they target our industry?
- ☑ How often has this specific attack been observed recently by organizations like ours?
- ☑ Is the trend up or down?
- ☑ Which vulnerabilities does this attack exploit, and are those vulnerabilities present in our organization?
- ☑ What kind of damage, technical and financial, has this attack caused in organizations like ours?

Threat analysts still need to know a great deal about the organization and its security defenses, but threat intelligence enriches their knowledge of attacks, the actors behind them, and their targets. It also provides hard data on the prevalence of the attacks.

Figures 8-2 and 8-3 show some of the forms the intelligence might take. Figure 8-2 lists the kinds of questions about a malware sample that a security intelligence solution answers for analysts.

Samsam Cyber attack

Add Reference to List... Report as Inaccurate
Share Event Hide This Event

- **Who is reported** together with Samsam?
- **What attackers are using** Samsam?
- **Who is targeted using** Samsam?
- **What operations are reported with** Samsam?
- **What technical indicators** are related to Samsam?
- **Which authors are reporting about** Samsam?

Figure 8-2: Questions about a malware sample that a security intelligence solution answers. (Source: Recorded Future)

76 | The Security Intelligence Handbook

Figure 8-3 shows trends in the proliferation of ransomware families.

The trend line to the right of each ransomware family indicates increasing or decreasing references across a huge range of threat data sources such as code repositories, paste sites, security research blogs, underground forums, and .onion (Tor accessible) forums. Additional information might be available about how the ransomware families connect to threat actors, targets, and exploit kits.

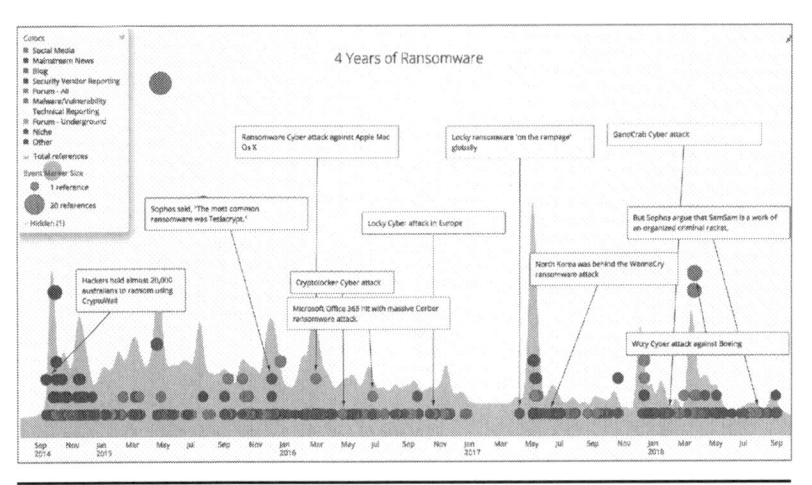

Figure 8-3: Timeline depicting the proliferation of new ransomware families. (Source: Recorded Future)

Security Intelligence and the Financial Cost of Attacks

The other major component of the formulas in our model is the probable cost of successful attacks. Most of the data for estimating cost is likely to come from inside the organization. However, security intelligence provides useful reference points on topics like:

- ☑ The cost of similar attacks on organizations of the same size and in the same industry
- ☑ The systems that need to be remediated after an attack, and the type of remediation they require

We will discuss risk management more in Chapter 12, including the Threat Category Risk (TCR) framework which was developed by Levi Gundert of Recorded Future, and is explained in detail in his book, "The Risk Business, What CISOs Need to Know About Risk-Based Cybersecurity."

Chapter 9

Third-Party Intelligence

In this chapter

- Explore the impact of increasing third-party risk
- Understand why static assessment of third-party risk falls short
- See why using real-time, automated security intelligence is the best way to mitigate third-party risk

"A chain is no stronger than its weakest link."

— Proverb

Third-Party Risk Looms Large

Because businesses and their supply chains are so tightly integrated, it's critical to consider the security of your partners, vendors, and other third parties when assessing the risk profile of your own organization.

A recent survey by the Ponemon Institute, "Digital Transformation & Cyber Risk: What You Need to Know to Stay Safe," found that 55 percent of organizations have had a breach that originated from a third party, and 53 percent say their tools for managing third-party risk are only somewhat effective or are not effective. These and related statistics are shown in Figure 9-1.

Third-Party Risk Is Real

55% of organizations have experienced a data breach originated from a third party

58% of organizations do not have a third-party cyber risk management program

53% of organizations say their tools for managing third-party risk are only somewhat effective or are not effective

What Recorded Future Knows About The World's Top Companies:

65% have **exposed** credentials

11% are being **discussed** on the **dark web**

44% are running **risky** technology

Figure 9-1: Most organizations are exposed to significant risks through their relationships with third parties. (Sources: Ponemon Institute and Recorded Future)

The writing is on the wall: Third-party attacks will continue to increase and get worse and will further complicate cyber risk management.

Traditional third-party risk assessment methods rely on static outputs, like self-assessments, financial audits, monthly reports about new vulnerabilities discovered in the systems an organization uses, and occasional reports on the status of security control compliance. All of these become outdated quickly, and they don't provide the comprehensive intelligence you need to make informed decisions about managing third-party risks to your organization.

In contrast, real-time security intelligence, specifically third-party intelligence, enables you to accurately assess risk posed by third parties and keep assessments current as conditions change and new threats emerge.

Traditional Risk Assessments Fall Short

Many of the most common third-party risk management practices employed today lag behind security requirements. Static assessments of risk — like financial audits and security certificate verifications — are still important, but they often lack context and timeliness.

Organizations following traditional approaches to managing third-party risk often use these three steps:

1. They attempt to understand their organization's business relationship with a third party and how it exposes their organization to threats.

2. Based on that understanding, they identify frameworks to evaluate the third party's financial health, corporate controls, and IT security and hygiene, as well as how these factors relate to their own organization's approach to security.

3. Using those frameworks, they assess the third party to determine whether it is compliant with security standards like SOC 2 or FISMA. Sometimes they conduct a financial audit of the third party.

While these steps are essential for evaluating third-party risk, they don't tell the whole story. The outputs are static and cannot reflect quickly changing conditions and emerging threats. The analysis is often too simplistic to produce actionable recommendations. Sometimes, the final report is opaque, making it impossible to dig deeper into the methodology behind the analysis. All of these factors create blind spots that leave decision-makers unsure whether crucial pieces of information might have been overlooked.

TIP When assessing third-party risk, do not rely entirely on self-reporting questionnaires or a vendor's inwardly focused view of their own security defenses. Round these out with an external, unbiased perspective on the vendor's threat landscape.

> **A Thought Experiment**
>
> Imagine that you went through the traditional steps of a static risk assessment, as outlined above. You concluded that one vendor in your supply chain is safe to work with.
>
> Now, this supplier experiences a data breach that may or may not have exposed your organization's internal data. Are you able to accurately determine what, if any, proactive security measures you need to take and how quickly you need to act?

Three Things to Look for in Security Intelligence

To accurately evaluate third-party risk in real time, you need a solution that offers immediate context on the current threat landscape. Security intelligence — delivered in the form of third-party intelligence — provides critical context that enables you to determine which shortcomings in your supply-chain partners' defenses represent meaningful risks to your organization. Those include not only the risks present at the time of assessment, but also current risks and a historical view — which provide even more context to detect, prevent, and resolve risks.

To effectively evaluate third-party risk, a third-party intelligence solution needs to offer:

1. Automation and analytics to quickly and comprehensively sort massive amounts of data
2. Real-time alerts on threats and changes to risks
3. Ongoing visibility into your partners' ever-changing threat environments

Automation and analytics

To manage risk for your organization, you need access to massive amounts of threat data from a wide variety of sources across the open web, the dark web, as well as technical and news sources and discussion forums. The same applies to assessing risks introduced by the third parties in your supply chain.

However, given the scale of cybersecurity-related content from these sources, totaling billions of facts, you need a third-party intelligence solution that uses automation and algorithms to collect and analyze these details. It must be able to:

- ☑ Analyze, classify, connect, fuse, and index data points using natural language processing and multiple analytical models
- ☑ Generate objective, data-driven risk scores using a straightforward formula
- ☑ Provide clear, accessible evidence for the risk scores it assigns

Real-time updates to risk scores

Static assessments quickly become outdated. Weekly or monthly intelligence reports produced by human analysts provide essential overviews, but often arrive too late to enable effective action. Risk scoring is much more effective when it updates in real time and draws on a large pool of sources. These capabilities make risk scores much more reliable for making immediate assessments and reaching security decisions.

For example, a trading partner might generally be regarded as low risk based on standard reporting. However, let's say the partner suffers a data breach that may or may not affect your organization. If you rely solely on static risk assessments, you likely won't know the breach happened in the first place — or you'll find out too late. You may have to wait too long to acquire the intelligence needed to accurately evaluate the risk. What was the cause of the breach? Was it an exploited vulnerability in a system used by the partner? A social engineering attack? Static assessments alone do not provide the evidence required to justify asking that third party to put additional security controls in place.

If you want to boost the effectiveness of your third-party risk program, start by thinking critically about five key questions:

1. Who are my most critical vendors?
2. What am I legally accountable for?

3. What is my current vendor risk assessment process?
4. Who else in my organization needs this information?
5. How does the global threat landscape affect my partners?

ON THE WEB

To learn more about these questions, and how to go about answering them, read the Recorded Future e-book, "Closing the Visibility Gap: 5 Questions to Ask Yourself About Your Third-Party Risk."

Transparent risk assessments

What's the point of a risk assessment if you can't use it to get your third parties to take action?

Information without context leaves us like Cassandra in Greek mythology. In a bid for her love, the god Apollo gave her the gift of prophecy, but still she scorned his romantic advances. In his anger, Apollo let her keep her foresight, but he cursed her so that nobody would ever believe her warnings about the future.

Many risk assessments today suffer the same fate as Cassandra's prophecies. When we rely on vague scoring methods or opaque sourcing, our advice is hard to accept, even if it's accurate. Too often, organizations fail to act on intelligence because leaders don't understand it or don't know the source.

A security intelligence solution must show the risk rules that are triggered by an alert — and be transparent about its sources (Figure 9-2). This enables security professionals to see for themselves why something like an alert on a particular IP address might represent a real risk. The extra detail also eliminates the suspicion that information might have been overlooked. This context allows for faster due diligence and reference checking, including when evaluating static assessments.

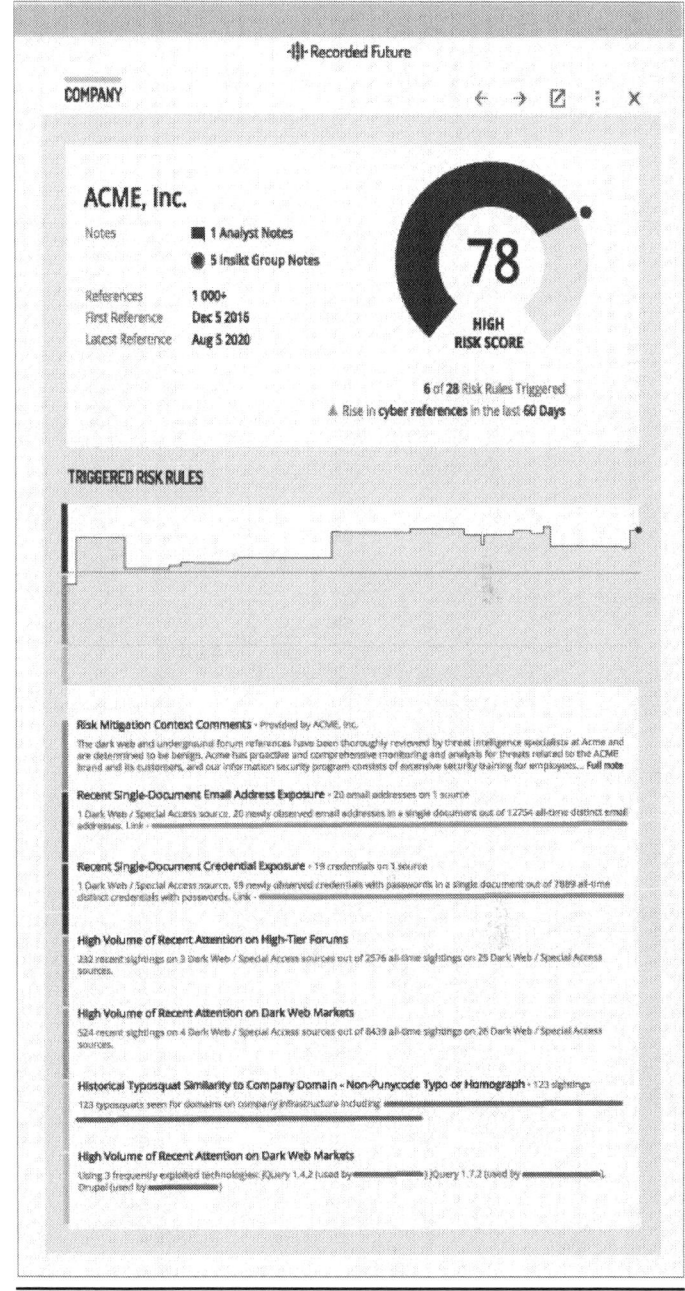

Figure 9-2: Third-party intelligence provides context for identifying shortcomings in the defenses of supply-chain partners.

Responding to High Third-Party Risk Scores

What do you do when faced with high risk scores for a third party? Not every data breach justifies terminating business with that partner. Just about every organization contends with cyberattacks and unexpected downtime, and partners are no exception. The more important issue is how they (and you) deal with incidents and take steps to reduce future risks.

A change in risk scores may present an opportunity to talk with your business partners about their approach to security. On your end, it's important to look more closely at whether the risk rules that were triggered will impact your organization's network. For example, a partner's risk score might increase because typosquatting websites closely resembling legitimate websites operated by the partner were discovered. Putting those sites on the deny list in your own network is one way to thwart phishing campaigns while you investigate what steps that partner plans to take to protect its brand identity.

For smart security decisions that involve your third parties, you need up-to-the-minute context and evidence provided by third-party intelligence.

Case Study: Insurance Company Gains Real-Time View of Third-Party Risk

For years, a *Fortune* 100 insurance company struggled to maintain a clear and current view of the risk profiles of its partners. The solution this organization relied on used data that was often outdated and rarely refreshed. The company wasn't able to see how a partner's risk score was trending over time, and they lacked visibility into specific events that were impacting the score.

This insurance company adopted a security intelligence solution from Recorded Future that includes third-party intelligence. This intelligence enables its security team to better understand, analyze, and rapidly address third-party risks, including:

- Corporate emails, credentials, and company mentions found on the dark web
- Negative social media chatter
- Domain abuse (often indicative of phishing attacks)
- Use of vulnerable technologies
- IT infrastructure misuse or abuse

The leader of the insurance company's third-party information risk management team says, "[Third-party intelligence provides] valuable insights into the risk postures of the critical suppliers we do business with — from real-time risk scores and alerts to custom rules we've set — and allows us to drill deeper when needed." By prioritizing security intelligence, the Recorded Future solution empowers the team to quickly:

- Rule out low-risk alerts and false positives
- Focus on the most significant threats
- Take immediate action to resolve them

This solution has enabled the company to reduce time spent on due diligence and reference checking by 50 percent, and replace a static, point-in-time approach with continuous monitoring.

Read the full case study at https://go.recordedfuture.com/hubfs/insurance-case-study.pdf.

Chapter 10

Brand Intelligence

In this chapter

- Review the many forms of digital risk to brands
- Learn how security intelligence identifies and remediates online attacks against brands

"Every contact leaves a trace."

— Locard's exchange principle of forensic science

Brand protection involves safeguarding an organization's image, reputation, and customers from attacks that primarily never touch its network or systems. These threats include:

- ☑ Fake websites and social media accounts used to impersonate the organization or its employees for fraud and phishing attacks
- ☑ Malicious content and false information about the organization and its products posted on websites and social media platforms
- ☑ Counterfeit products and software offered in digital marketplaces and app stores
- ☑ Data leaks and leaked credentials from employees and executives

Most of these threats are posed by financially motivated criminals, but they may also involve hacktivists, dissatisfied customers, competitors, and careless or disgruntled employees who reveal information online.

Protect Your Brand and Your Customers

To truly protect your brand, you need to be concerned about threats that leverage it to harm or influence your customers. Customers who are lured into a scam or fraud from an imitation of your website may hold your organization responsible. Those who buy a low-quality, counterfeit version of your product from an online marketplace may lose trust in your brand. Those who think one of your executives has published offensive content on the web may boycott your products — even if it wasn't your executive who posted it. Pleading "it wasn't our fault" won't restore their trust or your reputation in any of these scenarios.

A Different Kind of Detection

Most of the activities we have been discussing in this handbook involve creating intelligence about attackers and their tools. Brand intelligence includes some of that, as well, but the emphasis is instead on detecting your organization's name and brand everywhere they occur across the internet.

You need to be rigorous about listing and searching for mentions of all your brand and product names, and keywords that are associated with them. These include the names of:

- ☑ Your parent organization
- ☑ Subsidiaries and business units
- ☑ Products
- ☑ Executives
- ☑ Managers and employees who engage with the public in web forums and via social media

It also includes trademarks, service marks, and advertising slogans that appear on your organization's authorized websites, since these are frequently used on phony websites.

Uncovering Evidence of Brand Impersonation and Abuse

Knowing what to look for empowers you to find evidence of brand impersonation and abuse in places many organizations never search. For example, a brand intelligence solution enables you to:

- ☑ Search domain registries to find domain names that include your organization or product name, or variations of them
- ☑ Crawl the web to find typosquatting domains
- ☑ Monitor social media to alert you to hashtags that include your organization or product name, or variations of them
- ☑ Scan social media to detect accounts that claim to belong to your organization, your executives, or your employees
- ☑ Check app stores to uncover unauthorized mobile apps using your branding
- ☑ Comb web forums for threat actors planning to impersonate your brand

Use case: Typosquatting and fraudulent domains

Typosquatting involves manipulating the characters in an organization's domain name into nearly identical domains. For instance, threat actors targeting example.com might create a typosquat URL of exanple.com. Attackers often register thousands of domains differing by a single character from their target organizations' URLs. They do this for reasons ranging from suspicious to fully malicious.

Rogue websites using these modified domain names are built to look like legitimate websites. The rogue domains and websites are often used in spear-phishing campaigns against employees or customers, watering-hole attacks, and drive-by download attacks.

Being alerted to newly registered phishing and typosquatting domains in real time is the best way to narrow the window of opportunity for threat actors to impersonate your brand and defraud unsuspecting users. Once the malicious infrastructure is identified, you're able to employ a takedown service to nullify the threat.

Uncovering Evidence of Breaches on the Web

By monitoring the web — including private forums on the dark web — brand intelligence solutions enable you to uncover evidence of data breaches within your organization and partner ecosystem. You may find:

- ☑ Your customers' names and data
- ☑ Financial account data and Social Security numbers
- ☑ Leaked or stolen credentials from your employees
- ☑ Paste and bin sites containing your proprietary software code
- ☑ Forums mentioning your organization and announcing intentions to attack it
- ☑ Forums selling tools and discussing techniques to attack organizations like yours

Timely discovery of these indicators enables you to:

- ☑ Secure the sources of the data
- ☑ Find and fix vulnerabilities and misconfigurations in your infrastructure
- ☑ Mitigate future risks by improving security controls
- ☑ Identify ways to improve employee training and coding practices
- ☑ Enable your SecOps and incident response teams to recognize attacks faster

Chapter 10: Brand Intelligence | 93

> **TIP**
>
> It's often possible to narrow down the source of a leak by looking at exactly what information and artifacts are found on the web, where they are found, and what else is found in the same place. For example, if you find product designs or software code on a dark web site and recognize that they were shared with only a few suppliers, you would know to investigate the security controls of those suppliers as part of your third-party risk management program. If your organization's name was mentioned on a hacker's forum whose members are known to attack certain applications, you could increase protection of the targeted applications by patching the systems they run on, monitoring them more closely, and adding security controls.

Use case: Compromised data

Threat actors make money from many types of compromised personal information and corporate intellectual property. Examples of compromised data for sale on the dark web include medical records, cloned and compromised gift cards, and stolen credentials to "pay for" services like Netflix and Uber, and items charged via PayPal, as illustrated in Figure 10-1.

```
Credential leak targeting ▓▓▓▓@gmail.com, ▓▓▓▓@yahoo.co.uk, ▓▓▓▓@live.com
▓▓▓▓ Много всего! Раздача с папок
2015   Translated from Russian: "2015 ▓▓▓▓ @gmx.de : sol123779 Deezer ▓▓▓▓ @hotmail.com : pin2806 | Deezer ... Cru
       nchyroll privato ▓▓▓▓ @gmail.com : spartan303 Spotify ▓▓▓▓ @hotmail.co.uk : jurassic5 | Premium, GB ▓▓▓▓ @ y
       ahoo.co.uk : plasticman4972 | Premium, GB Netflix ▓▓▓▓ @live.com : Peru !" Forum Thread
       Show original
       Source  ▓▓▓▓  Forum by SimpsoniBart on Aug 31, 2018, 18:29
              ▓▓▓▓ • Reference Actions • 1+ reference
```

Figure 10-1: Compromised data – Spotify credentials disclosed on the dark web. (Source: Recorded Future)

A high percentage of hacking-related breaches leverage stolen or weak passwords. Threat actors regularly upload massive caches of usernames and passwords to paste sites and the dark web, or make them available for sale on underground marketplaces. These data dumps may include corporate email addresses and passwords, as well as login details for other sites.

Monitoring external sources for this type of intelligence will dramatically increase your visibility — not just into leaked credentials, but also into potential breaches of corporate data and proprietary code.

Disinformation is Alarmingly Simple and Inexpensive

Spreading lies about an organization on the web is easy and cheap. As a learning exercise, Recorded Future's Insikt Group® used a disinformation service provider to launch a negative campaign against a fictional corporation for just $4,200.

The exercise

Insikt Group created a fictitious company. It then found two disinformation service providers on Russian-speaking underground forums and commissioned them to generate intentionally false narratives across the web. One was asked to create positive propaganda to make the company seem appealing. The other was tasked with spreading malicious material accusing the same company of unethical business practices.

The results

Insikt Group discovered that launching disinformation campaigns is alarmingly simple and inexpensive. Both misinformation campaigns produced results in less than a month for only a few thousand dollars: $1,850 for the positive propaganda effort and $4,200 for the negative disinformation campaign. The service providers disseminated their messages successfully by placing articles on reputable web sites and creating social media accounts of seemingly real people.

The conclusions

- Disinformation services are publicly available on underground forums.

- For a few thousand dollars, disinformation service providers will publish articles in media sources ranging from dubious websites to reputable news outlets.

- These service providers use a combination of established and new social media accounts to propagate content without triggering content moderation controls.

Learn about the methods used by disinformation service providers in Insikt Group's cyber threat analysis report: "The Price of Influence: Disinformation in the Private Sector."

Critical Qualities for Security Intelligence Solutions

Of course, mitigating digital risk to your brand is not simply a matter of stumbling across one typosquatting domain or some isolated piece of stolen data. Somebody, or something, has to do the broader work of collecting masses of data, sifting through thousands of data points, analyzing relationships among the data points, deciding priorities, and ultimately taking action.

The best approach is to use a brand intelligence solution that:

- ☑ **Collects and scans data from the broadest range and variety of sources**: Automation at the data-collection stage saves analysts precious time. The best solutions gather data not only from open web sources, but also from the dark web and technical sources.

- ☑ **Maps, monitors, and scores brand risk**: Through automation, advanced data science, and analytical techniques like natural language processing, effective brand intelligence tools enable analysts to link business attributes with related digital assets and detect, score, and prioritize events related to brand risk.

- ☑ **Coordinates remediation**: Robust brand intelligence solutions generate alerts and reports that provide information on how to remediate problems. They also integrate with tools that perform remediation immediately and with service providers that take down instances of domain abuse.

Case Study: Defeating Typosquatting at a Large HR Solutions Provider

A large human resources, health, and wealth benefits services provider enables other organizations to manage their human resources. This company handles a lot of personally identifiable information (PII) — including sensitive health and financial data. To protect that data, they have an extensive security operations center, featuring 24/7/365 monitoring, incident response, investigation and forensics, and more.

Their vice president of security operations says that at one time it took a team of around 100 people to manage these functions. With Recorded Future, it takes 10. "Obtaining a list of all the mentions of our company across the internet by the end of the day was totally infeasible, even if I had 10 or 20 people working on it," the VP says.

The VP adds, "Sure, we could spend a lot of money to get people burner accounts and access to these private spaces, but what a waste! Anything beyond two people makes no sense compared to just using Recorded Future. The cost is less than two headcount, versus the 10 or 20 I would need to try to do something similar."

For example, one morning an alert went off about a potential typosquatting domain. The alert was triggered by a monitoring rule the team had set up in Recorded Future to check for fraudulent domains that resemble ones owned by the organization. Registering these domains is often the first step in a phishing attack.

As soon as the team got the alert, they investigated and found phishing attempts targeting their organization and some of their clients. They immediately sent out a flash report to their whole organization and all their clients and partners. The report provided actionable recommendations on how to counter the attack: Block the domain at your proxy and use event logs to scan for the threat with your SIEM. Many of their partners reported hits from the site, but they were able to block access before any damage was done.

Thanks to real-time brand intelligence, the company was able to mitigate the threat in a matter of hours, rather than weeks — or never.

Chapter 11

Geopolitical Intelligence

In this chapter

- Understand the factors that cause geopolitical risk
- Discover all the groups that use geopolitical intelligence
- Explore geofencing and geopolitical risk event types

"One city gives you gifts, another robs you... Cities and countries are as alive, as feeling, as fickle and uncertain as people."

— Roman Payne

What Is Geopolitical Risk?

Geopolitical risk is exposure to location-specific events.

Think about a country or city where your organization has an office or a facility such as a factory, an office, a warehouse, or perhaps a clinic or a consulate. The operations of that facility could be affected by:

- ☑ Decisions and actions by government bodies and agencies — from passing legislation, to introducing regulations, to mobilizing police or military forces in a state of emergency
- ☑ Actions by political parties, trade unions, activist groups, and other organizations — including strikes, demonstrations, protests, boycotts, social media campaigns, and even riots and targeted attacks on physical locations and property

☑ Natural and man-made disasters — such as disease outbreaks, hurricanes and earthquakes, military actions, and terrorist attacks

The effects of these events range from temporary disruptions, to millions of dollars in direct and indirect costs, to loss of life.

High Impact

In a recent survey of global organizations with revenue of $250 million or more, about 90 percent of executives from companies in the Americas say country-level and geopolitical risk have a high or very high impact. Worldwide, 70 percent of the executives say their company has an individual or function responsible for political risk management.

The authors of the study highlighted four types of political risk:

- Risks arising from conflicts between countries and changes in international systems

- Risks related to national political environments, the stability of governments and institutions, and legislation

- Risks that emerge when governments change environmental, health and safety, financial market, and other regulations

- Risks created by activism on the part of groups such as trade unions and consumer bodies

Source: EY, "Geostrategy in Practice 2020," May 2020.

Geopolitical Intelligence

Consider the advantages of being warned days before these types of events impact your organization, or being alerted in real time when they occur. That knowledge may enable you to prevent the events from affecting your organization — or it might put you in a position to respond faster when mitigating their effect.

Additionally, intelligence about local attitudes and long-term trends provides the insights you need to make smarter determinations about expanding operations into specific countries and cities.

Location, location, location

Geopolitical intelligence uses the security intelligence lifecycle described in Chapter 3. The main difference between geopolitical intelligence and other types of security intelligence is the starting point.

Security intelligence activities for security operations, incident response, vulnerability management, threat analysis, and third-party risk teams are organized primarily around threats and threat actors. Brand intelligence focuses on names and keywords related to the organization's brands and products.

In contrast, geopolitical intelligence starts with geographical locations — typically the cities, countries, and regions where your organization has physical assets and facilities. Its output is facts and insights about location-specific events that have a potential impact on the operations of those facilities and the staff there.

Supply chains, customers, and geopolitical risk

Geopolitical risk is not just about your organization's offices and facilities. As illustrated in 2020, during the early phases of the COVID-19 pandemic, disruptions that affect supply-chain partners and transportation networks also have a dramatic effect on the operations of an organization. This is true even in regions where the organization has no physical assets or personnel. When location-specific events affect a large number of its customers or clients, an organization may struggle as a result.

Who Uses Geopolitical Intelligence?

Geopolitical intelligence is valuable to many groups within organizations that are global or aspire to expand globally. The names of the groups often differ across various organizations, but may include the following teams:

- ☑ Physical security
- ☑ Security operations

- ☑ Business continuity
- ☑ Supply-chain management
- ☑ Risk management
- ☑ Government relations
- ☑ Public policy or public affairs
- ☑ Office of the general counsel
- ☑ Regional and national management

These groups have a variety of responsibilities related to geopolitical risks, including:

- ☑ Anticipating and preventing harm (e.g., closing a facility before a mass demonstration)
- ☑ Responding quickly to mitigate the effects of events (e.g., providing aid to employees or finding alternate sources of supply after a natural disaster)
- ☑ Communicating key facts to employees, customers, business partners, and government agencies
- ☑ Assessing location-based risks in the future to guide investment and expansion decisions

DON'T FORGET To get the most out of geopolitical intelligence, consult with these groups about their information needs, and use that input to set priorities for intelligence collection and analysis. Tailor your output to be easily understood and actionable by these audiences. See the "Direction" and "Dissemination" sections of the security intelligence lifecycle discussion in Chapter 3.

Data Collection With Geofencing

To empower your organization to anticipate and cope with location-specific events, you need to start by selecting the locations and types of events that matter to your organization. The geopolitical intelligence solution will then monitor and filter data by location, which is called "geofencing."

TIP If your organization has a physical security or business continuity department, that team likely maintains a list of all of your office and facility locations around the world.

DON'T FORGET Dig even deeper than your list of offices and facilities by asking different groups in your organization about supply-chain partners, transportation networks, clients and customers, and other entities that may affect your operations. Document the locations where they might be susceptible to geopolitical events, and monitor them.

You also need to specify the event types to monitor. Figure 11-1 is an example of high-level geopolitical event categories and some of the specific items that might be offered within one category.

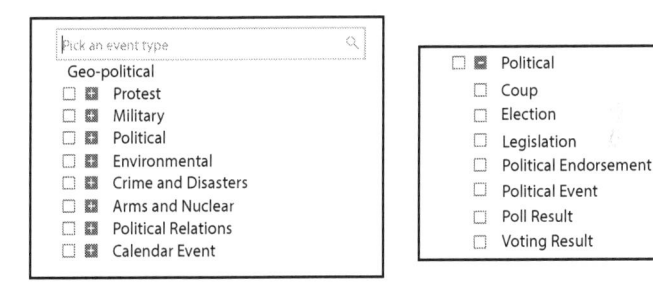

```
Pick an event type
Geo-political
  ☐ ⊞ Protest
  ☐ ⊞ Military
  ☐ ⊞ Political
  ☐ ⊞ Environmental
  ☐ ⊞ Crime and Disasters
  ☐ ⊞ Arms and Nuclear
  ☐ ⊞ Political Relations
  ☐ ⊞ Calendar Event
```

```
  ☐ ☑ Political
  ☐   Coup
  ☐   Election
  ☐   Legislation
  ☐   Political Endorsement
  ☐   Political Event
  ☐   Poll Result
  ☐   Voting Result
```

Figure 11-1: Examples of geopolitical event categories and the specific items within one category. (Source: Recorded Future)

Data and Information Sources

The sources of data and information used to produce geopolitical intelligence overlap with those used for other types of security intelligence. Technical sources such as threat feeds typically play a smaller role in geopolitical intelligence, because most cyber threats are not location-specific. The most valuable geopolitical intelligence sources tend to be specific to a country or city, for example:

- ☑ News and public media websites
- ☑ Social media posts

- ☑ Blogs
- ☑ Forums and marketplaces on both the open and dark web

Most of these sources include data and information from national and local governments, regulatory agencies, media organizations, trade unions, consumer groups, and individuals. However, activists and criminals also use the dark web to plan dangerous and illegal activities targeting specific locations — making dark web sources valuable for geopolitical intelligence.

Automation, Analytics, and Expertise

It takes an enormous amount of work to determine which sites, and which specific articles, videos, messages, and posts are relevant to a particular location and threat type. That's why organizations that are serious about managing geopolitical risk must use a security intelligence platform that combines analytics, automation, and human expertise to process and analyze data and information.

Automation reduces, and often eliminates, resource-intensive, time-consuming manual research. It also speeds up processes for calculating and updating risk scores, disseminating alerts, creating visual representations of data, and many additional tasks.

Analytics are what enable a security intelligence solution to collect millions of pieces of information from open web, dark web, and technical sources, and dynamically link and categorize them to generate intelligence about specified locations and geopolitical event types. Thanks to analytics, analysts don't need to manually comb through massive volumes of content, discover patterns, and connect the dots between facts and insights related to specific locations and threat types.

Specialized analytic tools assist in other areas as well. While most communication among threat actors is conducted in either English or Russian, government announcements, news stories, and social media and blog posts are naturally written in a variety of local languages. Natural language processing (NLP) is an analytic tool that identifies pieces of content that contain key words and phrases in every language. For example, NLP enables a security intelligence solution to find relevant news articles, blog posts, and dark web chatter related to a message in a Russian-language forum that mentions "В Киеве будет протестный марш" (a protest march in Kiev).

Of course, security intelligence is not just about automation and analytics. Often, there is no substitute for human expertise. This is particularly true when addressing issues related to specific regions and countries, where language skills (including knowledge of local slang) and familiarity with history and politics are critical. That is why you should also evaluate security intelligence solutions on their ability to deliver finished intelligence — especially finished geopolitical intelligence.

Finished intelligence may include custom research reports evaluating risks in specific regions, tailored insights about the latest threats affecting those areas, and hunting packages that accelerate the research of your incident response, threat hunting, and geopolitical risk teams.

TECH TALK For a technical discussion of how a security intelligence platform combines analytics with human expertise and automation to categorize and connect huge volumes of security data, read the Recorded Future white paper, "The Security Intelligence Graph: Inside Recorded Future's Methodology and Patented Technology."

Interacting With Geopolitical Intelligence

Security intelligence solutions enable you to access and interact with geopolitical intelligence in several formats, such as:

- ☑ Dashboards and maps showing risk levels by country and city
- ☑ Alerts triggered by events or changes in risk scores
- ☑ Reports detailing events and issues related to specified locations
- ☑ Background documents and insights summarizing key findings for countries and cities

In addition, some security intelligence solutions integrate with security tools like SIEMs and ticketing systems and use geographical tags to ensure that people concerned with specific cities, countries, and regions receive immediate alerts of events there.

Figure 11-2 is an example of a geopolitical intelligence dashboard that highlights high-risk areas on a map of the world.

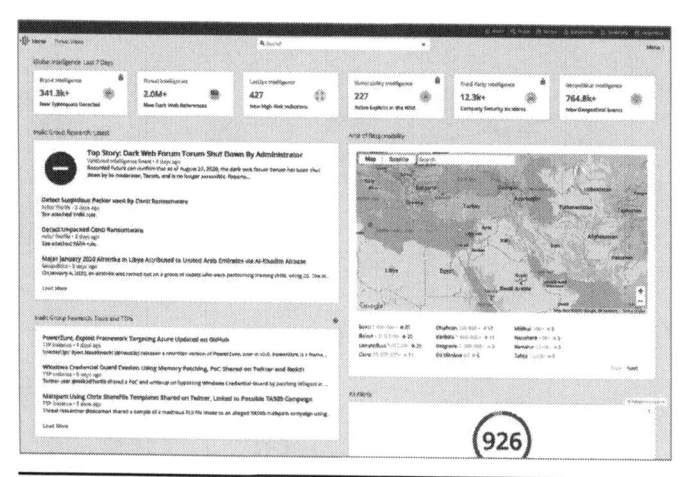

Figure 11-2: Example of a dashboard that highlights high-risk areas. (Source: Recorded Future)

Geopolitics and Cyber Threats

This chapter has focused on threats and events that originate in the same countries as the facilities you want to protect. However, geopolitical risk also involves, well, geopolitics: Political, economic, and ideological conflicts between nations and global alliances.

In the last several years the world has witnessed cyber attacks against internet, financial, and physical infrastructures. Among these have been attempts to overload or disable the websites of government agencies, non-governmental organizations (NGOs), and independent media outlets; as well as misinformation campaigns targeting governments, elections, and businesses.

Most of these attacks have been attributed to mysterious hacking groups, sometimes linked to governments, and occasionally even to departments of a government or a military service. Many government agencies, commercial businesses, and NGOs are caught in the crossfire — even when they have little or no connection to the dispute between nations that started the conflict.

Defending your organization against these types of threats requires a comprehensive security intelligence program that encompasses all of the topics discussed in this handbook, from SecOps and threat intelligence to brand protection, and from vulnerability and third-party risk management to geopolitical intelligence.

ON THE WEB To learn more about the link between geopolitical conflicts and cyber threats, read the Recorded Future blog post, "Geopolitics: An Overlooked Influencer in Cyber Operations." To find out more about the connection between national rivalries and hacktivism, read, "Return to Normalcy: False Flags and the Decline of International Hacktivism."

Chapter 12

Security Intelligence for Security Leaders

In this chapter

- See how security intelligence supports risk management and investments in cybersecurity programs
- Explore the types of security intelligence CISOs find most valuable
- Review how security intelligence mitigates the security skills gap

"An investment in knowledge pays the best interest."

— Benjamin Franklin

The job of the CISO has seen dramatic shifts in recent years. It once centered on making decisions about purchasing and implementing security technologies. Now, CISOs are far more likely to interact with the CEO and the board and to perform delicate balancing acts of pre-empting risk while ensuring business continuity. Security leaders need to be able to:

- ☑ Assess business and technical risks, including emerging threats and "known unknowns," that might impact the business
- ☑ Identify the right strategies and technologies to mitigate risks
- ☑ Communicate the nature of risks to top management and justify security investments based on financial value to the business

Security intelligence is a critical resource for all of these activities.

Risk Management

Perhaps the greatest responsibility of the modern CISO is risk management. This involves allocating resources and budget to minimize the likely impact of threats on the business. Figure 12-1 outlines the stages security leaders often move through when approaching this challenge.

Assess Security Requirements	Understand business and IT objectives and define responsibilities for the security function.
Assess Existing Security Protocols	Analyze current security people, processes, and technologies to develop an accurate picture of the security function.
Develop Initiatives	Using a risk-based approach, identify the most significant gaps in security, then define and prioritize initiatives to address them.
Track Progress	Continually monitor progress and ensure the security function is improving in line with requirements. Develop metrics to measure ongoing effectiveness.

Figure 12-1: A standard approach to assessing risk and developing a security strategy.

Internal data is not enough

The approach to security outlined in Figure 12-1 is dependent on having good intelligence about relevant risk factors and potential weaknesses in existing security programs. However, too often this kind of intelligence is only gathered from internal audits, known issues, and previous security incidents. That approach produces a list of challenges that have already affected your organization, but leaves out challenges that are on the horizon and haven't yet reached you.

External context is necessary to:

- ☑ Verify risk that's related to known problems
- ☑ Warn about emerging and unforeseen threats

Internal network traffic data, event logs, and alerting obviously bring value to risk management, but they don't provide enough context to build a comprehensive risk profile — and certainly not enough to define an entire strategy. Security professionals must be proactive about uncovering unknown risks. Context is what enables security leaders to determine which potential threats are most likely to become actual threats to their organization.

Sharpening the focus

Security intelligence provides context on general trends such as:

- ☑ The types of attacks that are becoming more (or less) frequent
- ☑ The types of attacks that are most costly to the victims
- ☑ TTPs of new threat actors who are coming forward, and the assets and organizations they are targeting
- ☑ The security practices and technologies that have proven the most (or least) successful in stopping or mitigating these attacks

Data and information on these trends allow security organizations to anticipate which threats will be the hot news items of tomorrow. However, contextualized external security intelligence is much more powerful. For example, it enables security groups to assess whether an emerging threat is *likely* to affect their specific organization based on factors like:

- ☑ **Industry**: Is the threat affecting other businesses in our vertical?
- ☑ **Technology**: Does the threat involve compromising software, hardware, or other technologies used in our organization?
- ☑ **Geography**: Does the threat target facilities in regions where we operate?
- ☑ **Attack method**: Have techniques used in the attack (including social engineering and technical methods) been used successfully against our organization or similar ones?

Without a depth of intelligence gathered from an extremely broad set of external data sources, it is impossible for security decision-makers to gain a holistic view of the cyber risk landscape and identify the greatest risks to their organization.

Figure 12-2 illustrates how a customized security intelligence dashboard highlights intelligence that is most relevant to a specific organization.

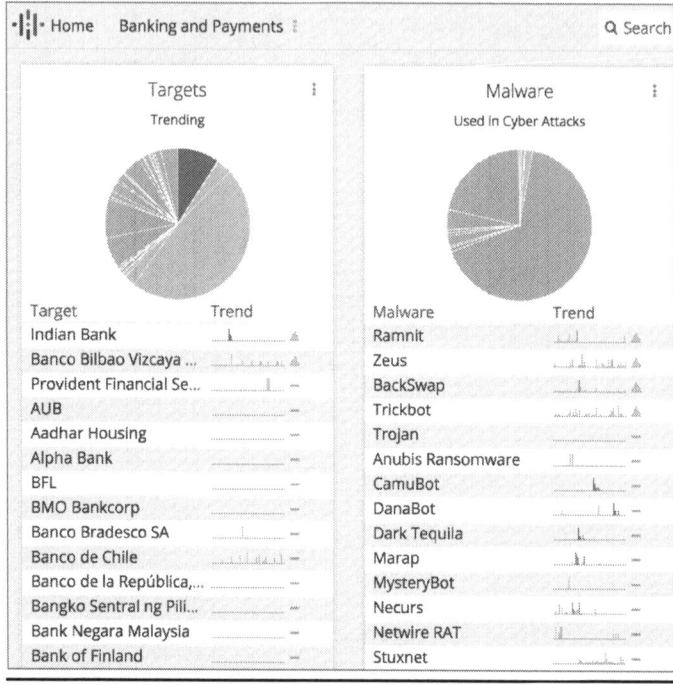

Targets Trending		Malware Used in Cyber Attacks	
Target	Trend	Malware	Trend
Indian Bank		Ramnit	
Banco Bilbao Vizcaya ...		Zeus	
Provident Financial Se...		BackSwap	
AUB		Trickbot	
Aadhar Housing		Trojan	
Alpha Bank		Anubis Ransomware	
BFL		CamuBot	
BMO Bankcorp		DanaBot	
Banco Bradesco SA		Dark Tequila	
Banco de Chile		Marap	
Banco de la República,...		MysteryBot	
Bangko Sentral ng Pili...		Necurs	
Bank Negara Malaysia		Netwire RAT	
Bank of Finland		Stuxnet	

Figure 12-2: A security intelligence dashboard pinpoints threats most relevant to a specific industry or technology. (Source: Recorded Future)

Mitigation: People, Processes, and Tools

Vulnerability scans and techniques such as penetration testing and red teaming contribute to a security team's ability to understand where gaps exist in their defenses. However, many organizations have far more technical vulnerabilities, more weaknesses in their security processes and policies, and more employees susceptible to social engineering than they could possibly patch, harden, and train in the immediate future.

Security intelligence enables security leaders to pinpoint the challenges that need to be addressed first by indicating:

- ☑ The threat actors most likely to target the organization
- ☑ The TTPs those threat actors use, and the weaknesses they tend to exploit

Early warnings

Analysts find threat actors on the dark web announcing their intention to attack specific industries, and even specific companies. Sometimes these threat actors use these platforms to recruit like-minded hackers to assist them. When monitoring dark web marketplaces, analysts are also able to track the development and sale of exploit kits targeting specific vulnerabilities and other hacker tools.

Security intelligence connects the dots across all of these entities to provide context on what they mean to your organization. And, as discussed earlier in this book, it is critical to focus on patching the vulnerabilities and mitigating the weaknesses that are actually at risk of being exploited before tackling others where exploitation is merely theoretical.

> **TIP** Use a security intelligence solution to scan the dark web and other sources for references to your organization, your industry, and specific technologies installed in your organization.

Investment

Deciding how to invest in cybersecurity has become a daunting challenge in recent times. Financial investment advisers Momentum Partners identified more than 3,500 companies in 2019 that specialize in cybersecurity technologies and services. With so many choices, how are CISOs supposed to identify the most effective solutions to implement as part of a proactive security strategy?

The only logical way is to make investment decisions based on risk. Each organization has its own unique risk profile, shaped by its industry, physical locations, and internal infrastructure. Security intelligence enables security leaders to understand the most pressing threats to their organization, making the tasks of identifying and justifying areas for investment much simpler. The end goal is to be able to judge that risk and make investments based upon sound knowledge of the threat landscape.

Communication

CISOs are often challenged by the need to describe threats and justify countermeasures in terms that will motivate non-technical business leaders, such as cost, ROI, impact on customers, and competitive advantages.

Bombarding senior stakeholders with news about every single threat is not a good option. Instead, security intelligence provides powerful insights for guiding these types of discussions, such as:

- ☑ The impacts of similar attacks on companies in the same industry, and on organizations of the same size in other industries
- ☑ Cyber trends and intelligence from the dark web indicating that the organization is likely to be targeted

Case Study: Security Intelligence and Automation at a Global Retailer

With nearly 3,600 stores and over 135,000 employees worldwide, one global retail chain faces challenges that run the gamut from loss and fraud prevention and corporate security to protecting customers' PII.

The retailer uses automation to centralize and customize security intelligence for every security function. Automation ensures that the real-time security intelligence going into its SIEM is accurate and highly contextual — and that the output is presented in flexible, easy-to-use formats.

The company's biggest return on investment — and the biggest advantage to managing its security intelligence through an all-in-one platform — is better relationships both across the cybersecurity teams and with other departments.

Says a senior manager at the company's cyber defense center: "None of us is operating in a silo. If we can use security intelligence to keep us safe, but also help our program visibility, that helps to make a business case for more capabilities. Having champions on other teams to back the benefits of security intelligence really helps our return on investment."

For a comprehensive analysis of the retail chain's cost savings and business benefits, read Forrester's report: "The Total Economic Impact™ Of Recorded Future."

Supporting Security Leaders

We have mentioned several times that security intelligence needs to be comprehensive, relevant, and contextualized to be useful to members of the security organization. When it comes to CISOs and other security leaders, it also needs to be concise and timely.

For example, security intelligence provides security leaders with a real-time picture of the latest threats, trends, and events. A user-friendly security intelligence dashboard (or some other "at-a-glance" format) enables security leaders to respond to a threat or communicate the potential impact of a new threat type to business leaders and board members.

DON'T FORGET Security intelligence is not just for SecOps teams and threat analysts. Security leaders are also key consumers of security intelligence. Think through the kinds of intelligence security leaders need on a daily basis (e.g., a dashboard and a list of key new intelligence findings from the previous day), at regular intervals (e.g., summaries and trends for a quarterly risk report), and for crises (e.g., intelligence about attacks that have just been detected), and make sure processes and security intelligence tools are in place to address all of these needs.

The Security Skills Gap

One of the responsibilities of a CISO is to make sure the security and IT organization is staffed with the right people to carry out its mission. Yet, the cybersecurity field has a widely publicized skills shortage, and existing security staff frequently find themselves under the pressure of unmanageable workloads.

Security intelligence provides a partial answer by automating the most labor-intensive, but critical, tasks in cybersecurity, which frees up people's time for the skill-intensive tasks for which they're trained. For example, security intelligence reduces the massive volume of alerts generated by SIEMs and other security tools, rapidly collects and correlates context from multiple sources, and provides the intelligence required to prioritize risks.

Making security intelligence available across all security functions saves a huge amount of time, as security operations and incident response teams, threat analysts, vulnerability management specialists, and other security personnel are provided the intelligence and context they need to make fast, confident decisions.

Powerful security intelligence also empowers more junior personnel to quickly upskill and perform above their experience level, so the CISO doesn't have to recruit as many senior practitioners.

Risk-Based Cybersecurity: A Better Way to Manage

Many cybersecurity teams are either threat driven or compliance driven. Threat-driven teams are focused on reacting to the latest high-profile threats — whether or not they pose an actual risk to the organization. Meanwhile, compliance-driven teams excel at checking the boxes of compliance standards and frameworks.

Neither of these maximize security, and both make it hard to have meaningful discussions with managers and executives who are far more interested in profit and loss than threats and compliance.

In his book, "The Risk Business, What CISOs Need to Know About Risk-Based Cybersecurity," Levi Gundert offers a better alternative. His concept, called "risk-based cybersecurity," posits that:

1. Risk is the possibility that an event will eventually lead to reduced profitability.

2. The risk of a cyber threat is quantifiable in monetary terms with relatively little effort.

3. The net impact of mitigation activities are able to be calculated by comparing the cost of mitigation with the expected savings from mitigating the risk.

4. These calculations enable security programs to select the activities that maximize positive impact on the profitability of the organization.

Did a flashing yellow warning light go off in your head at the words "with relatively little effort" in point number 2? Building on the work of Douglas W. Hubbard and Richard Seiersen, Gundert illustrates how to use estimation, simulation, and a Threat Category Risk (TCR) framework to easily quantify threats to an organization in monetary terms.

Beyond guiding security teams to the most effective allocation of resources and staff, risk-based security enables security leaders to communicate with executives in a language they understand and appreciate: The language of dollars and cents.

"The Risk Business, What CISOs Need to Know About Risk-Based Cybersecurity" is available for download at https://go.recordedfuture.com/the-risk-business. For additional information on how to quantify cybersecurity risk, read Hubbard's and Seiersen's book "How to Measure Anything in Cybersecurity Risk."

Section 3: Creating and Scaling Your Security Intelligence Program

Chapter 13

Analytical Frameworks for Security Intelligence

In this chapter

- Learn about the advantages of using intelligence frameworks
- Understand the strengths and weaknesses of the three best-known frameworks
- See how the three frameworks complement each other

"Structure is required for creativity."

— Twyla Tharp

Analytical intelligence frameworks provide structures for thinking about attacks and adversaries. They promote broad understanding of how attackers think, the TTPs they use, and where in an attack lifecycle specific events occur. This knowledge empowers defenders to take decisive action faster and stop attackers sooner.

Frameworks also focus attention on the details that require further investigation. This attention to detail ensures that threats have been fully removed, and that measures are put in place to prevent future intrusions of the same kind.

Finally, frameworks are useful for sharing information within and across organizations. They provide common grammar and syntax for explaining the details of attacks and how those details relate to each other. A shared framework makes it easier to ingest security intelligence from security intelligence vendors, open source forums, information sharing and analysis centers (ISACs), and other sources.

> **TIP** The frameworks outlined below are complementary, not competitive. You may choose to utilize any one, two, or all three of them.

The Lockheed Martin Cyber Kill Chain®

The Cyber Kill Chain®, first developed by Lockheed Martin in 2011, is the best known of the cybersecurity intelligence frameworks. It is based on the military concept of the kill chain, which breaks the structure of an attack into stages. By segmenting an attack, defenders are able to pinpoint which stage it is in and deploy appropriate countermeasures.

The Cyber Kill Chain describes seven stages of an attack:

1. Reconnaissance
2. Weaponization
3. Delivery
4. Exploitation
5. Installation
6. Command and Control
7. Actions on Objectives (sometimes referred to as exfiltration)

These stages are often laid out in a diagram similar to Figure 13-1.

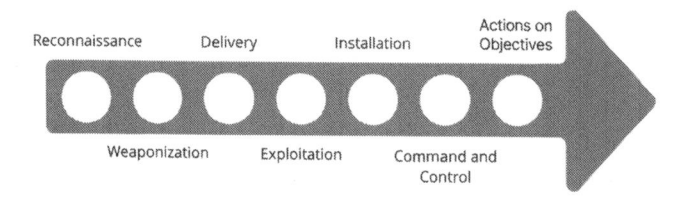

Figure 13-1: Diagram of Lockheed Martin's Cyber Kill Chain framework.

Security teams may choose to develop standard responses for each stage. For example, if you manage to stop an attack at the exploitation stage, you can have high confidence that nothing has been installed on the targeted systems, and full incident response activity may not be necessary.

The Cyber Kill Chain also allows organizations to build a defense-in-depth model that targets specific parts of the kill chain. For example, you might acquire intelligence specifically to monitor:

- ☑ References to your organization on the web that would indicate reconnaissance activities
- ☑ Information about weaponization against newly reported vulnerabilities in applications on your network

Limitations of the Cyber Kill Chain

The Cyber Kill Chain is a good way to start thinking about how to defend against attacks, but it has some limitations. One major criticism of this model is that it doesn't take into account the way many modern attacks work. For example, many phishing attacks skip the exploitation phase entirely, and instead rely on the victim to open a file with an embedded macro, or to double-click on an attached script.

However, even with its limitations, the Cyber Kill Chain creates a solid baseline to discuss attacks and where to stop them. It also makes it easier to share information about attacks within and outside of the organization using standard, well-defined attack points.

TECH TALK Find out more about the Cyber Kill Chain by reading the seminal white paper and visiting the Cyber Kill Chain website.

The Diamond Model

The Diamond Model was created in 2013 by researchers at the now-defunct Center for Cyber Intelligence Analysis and Threat Research (CCIATR). It is used to track attack groups over time, rather than the progress of individual attacks.

In its simplest form, the Diamond Model looks similar to Figure 13-2. It is used to classify the different elements of an attack. The diamond for an attacker or attack group is not static — it evolves as the attacker adjusts TTPs and changes infrastructure and targets.

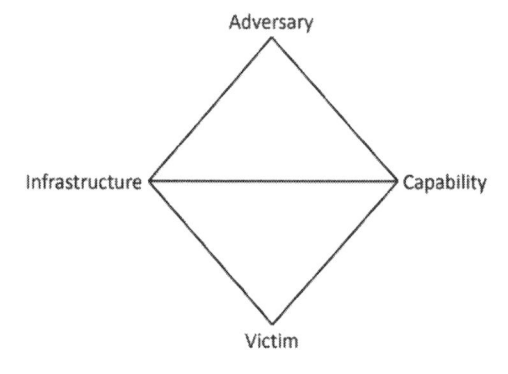

Figure 13-2: A simple Diamond Model design

The Diamond Model enables defenders to track an attacker, the victims, the attacker's capabilities, and the infrastructure the attacker uses. Each of the points on the diamond is a pivot point that defenders use during an investigation to connect one aspect of an attack with the others.

> **Pivoting**
>
> Let's say you uncover command and control traffic to a suspicious IP address. The Diamond Model would allow you to "pivot" from this initial indicator to find information about the attacker associated with that IP address, and then research the known capabilities of that attacker. Knowing those capabilities will enable you to respond to the incident more quickly and effectively. Or, imagine that your security intelligence solution uses the Diamond Model. If the board of directors asks who is launching similar attacks against other organizations in your industry (attribution), you may be able to quickly find a list of victims, the probable attacker, and a description of that attacker's TTPs. These will enable you to decide what defenses need to be put in place.

Flexibility

One of the biggest advantages of the Diamond Model is its flexibility and extensibility. You can add different aspects of an attack under the appropriate point on the diamond to create complex profiles of different attack groups. Other features of an attack that can be tracked include:

1. Phase
2. Result
3. Direction
4. Methodology
5. Resources

Drawbacks of the Diamond Model

The downside is that Diamond Models require a lot of maintenance. Some aspects of the model, especially infrastructure, change rapidly. If you don't update the diamond of an attacker constantly, you run the risk of working with outdated information. Even with these challenges, however, the Diamond Model can make the jobs of many security people easier by illustrating fast answers about evolving threats.

TIP Time stamp every update to a diamond so everybody using it has visibility into the age of the information.

TIP If you don't have the time and resources to manage this type of model yourself, you may be able to get updated information from a third-party intelligence provider.

ON THE WEB To learn more about the Diamond Model, read the Recorded Future blog post "Applying Security Intelligence to the Diamond Model of Intrusion Analysis", or download the original white paper "The Diamond Model of Intrusion Analysis."

The MITRE ATT&CK™ Framework

MITRE is a unique organization in the United States: A corporation responsible for managing federal funding for research projects across multiple federal agencies. It has had a huge impact on the security industry, including the development and maintenance of the Common Vulnerabilities and Exposures (CVE) and the Common Weakness Enumeration (CWE) databases.

MITRE has developed a number of other frameworks that are very important for security intelligence, including:

- ☑ The Trusted Automated Exchange of Intelligence Information (TAXII™) — a transport protocol that enables organizations to share intelligence over HTTPS and use common API commands to extract that intelligence
- ☑ Structured Threat Information eXpression (STIX™) — a standardized format for presenting intelligence
- ☑ The Cyber Observable eXpression (CybOX™) framework — a method for tracking observables from cybersecurity incidents

Categories of attacker behavior

The MITRE Adversarial Tactics, Techniques, and Common Knowledge (ATT&CK™) framework was created as a means of tracking adversarial behavior over time. ATT&CK builds on the Cyber Kill Chain, but rather than describing a single attack, it focuses on the indicators and tactics associated with specific adversaries.

ATT&CK uses 12 different tactic categories to describe adversary behavior:

1. Initial Access
2. Execution
3. Persistence
4. Privilege Escalation
5. Defense Evasion
6. Credential Access
7. Discovery
8. Lateral Movement
9. Collection
10. Command and Control
11. Exfiltration
12. Impact

Each of these tactical categories includes individual techniques that describe the adversary's behavior. For example, under the Initial Access category, behaviors include "Spearphishing Attachment," "Spearphishing Link," "Trusted Relationship," and "Valid Accounts."

ON THE WEB See the MITRE Enterprise ATT&CK Framework at https://attack.mitre.org/wiki/Main_Page.

This classification of behaviors allows security teams to be very granular in describing and tracking adversarial behavior, and it makes it easy to share information between teams.

ATT&CK is useful across a wide range of security functions, from security operations and threat analysis to incident response. Tracking adversary behavior in a structured and repeatable way enables teams to:

- ☑ Prioritize incident response
- ☑ Map indicators to attackers
- ☑ Identify holes in the organization's security posture

TIP: Intelligence frameworks may be used to standardize the way your security teams look at threats, indicators, vulnerabilities, and actors. If you are not prepared to build out your own framework for analysis, consider partnering with security companies that provide solutions built around existing frameworks. That approach enables you to enjoy the benefits of the framework and quickly improve the effectiveness of your security activities.

Chapter 14

Your Security Intelligence Journey

In this chapter

- Examine ways to clarify your security intelligence needs and goals
- Explore key success factors that contribute to effective programs
- Learn how to start simple and scale up

"No one was ever lost on a straight road."

— Proverb

In this chapter, we suggest some best practices for mapping out your security intelligence journey and building toward a comprehensive security intelligence program.

Don't Start With Threat Feeds

Many organizations begin their security intelligence programs by signing up for threat data feeds and connecting them with a SIEM solution. This may seem like a logical way to start because many threat data feeds are open source (i.e., free), and the technical indicators they deliver appear useful and easy to interpret. Since all malware is bad, and every suspicious URL could be used by an attacker, the more clues you have about them the better, right?

In reality, the vast majority of malware samples and suspicious URLs are not relevant to current threats to your organization. That's why feeding large volumes of unfiltered threat data to your SIEM will almost certainly create more alerts than answers — and ultimately, the kind of alert fatigue we examined in Chapter 4.

Clarify Your Security Intelligence Needs and Goals

Because security intelligence provides value to so many teams across your organization, it is important to develop priorities that accurately reflect the organization's overall needs and goals.

Answer these questions

Develop a clear set of goals by determining the needs of each security group in your organization and the advantages that security intelligence will provide for them.

Begin by considering these questions:

- ☑ What are your greatest risks?
- ☑ In what ways do you need security intelligence to address each of those risks?
- ☑ What is the potential impact of addressing each risk?
- ☑ What gaps need to be filled by information, technology, or people to make security intelligence effective in those areas?

ON THE WEB For a comprehensive look at the power of security intelligence, download "The Ultimate Security Intelligence Kit." This curated collection of white papers, reports, videos, podcasts, and more describes in detail how security intelligence works and all the ways it benefits your organization.

Identify which of your teams will benefit from security intelligence

Teams across your security organization will benefit from intelligence that drives informed decision-making and provides insightful perspectives. Intelligence that is comprehensive, relevant, and easy to consume has the potential to revolutionize how different roles in your organization operate day to day. When determining how to move your security intelligence strategy forward, it's important to identify all of the potential users in your organization and align the intelligence to their unique use cases.

DON'T FORGET Drill down into which outputs of security intelligence each group will use and exactly how they will benefit in terms of response times, cost savings, staff efficiency, investment decisions, etc. The needs and benefits are not always obvious. Documenting these details will enable you to set priorities, justify investments, and find new uses for security intelligence.

Key Success Factors

There are several factors that frequently contribute to effective security intelligence programs. The sooner you implement these, the faster you'll realize the full value of security intelligence.

Generating quick wins with monitoring

Monitoring security information often provides quick benefits with relatively modest investments. The key is to look for a few types of data that are particularly meaningful to your business and information security strategy for anticipating emerging threats and providing early warnings of actual attacks. These activities might include:

- ☑ Checking for new vulnerabilities that affect your most important software packages, servers, and endpoints
- ☑ Tracking threat trends that pose potential risks to your business operations
- ☑ Watching for any leaked corporate credentials, data, or code appearing on public or dark web sites
- ☑ Scanning the web and social media for the names of your organization and its brands, business units, and products

There are likely a few data types of vital importance to your business that are possible to monitor without investing in new infrastructure or staff. Doing so is likely to generate quick wins, demonstrate the advantages of security intelligence, and build enthusiasm for the program.

Ensuring that reports are useful

Many organizations get into the rut of producing daily reports that are of little to no use. Often these take the form of bulleted lists of detected threats with a simple low/medium/high impact rating. While these reports show that analysts are keeping busy and raising awareness of cyber threats across the organization, they typically have zero impact on operational outcomes.

Don't worry about producing reports on a schedule. Instead, make sure that every report and communication you do produce contains intelligence and insights that empower the affected parties to make decisions and take appropriate actions. Ideally, these will include at least basic information on:

- ☑ The probable threat actor(s)
- ☑ Techniques and tools used by the threat actor(s)
- ☑ Likely targets in the organization
- ☑ Whether the threat represents a real danger to the organization
- ☑ The likelihood that existing security controls are able to mitigate the threat
- ☑ Recommended actions to take in response

Automating as much as possible

Effective security intelligence programs typically focus on automation from the very beginning. They start by automating fundamental tasks like data aggregation, comparison, labeling, and contextualization. When these tasks are performed by machines, humans are freed up to focus on making effective and informed decisions.

As your security intelligence program becomes more sophisticated, you may find even more opportunities for automation. You will be able to automate information sharing among a larger group of security solutions and automate more workflows that provide intelligence to security operations and incident response teams, threat analysts, fraud prevention teams, vulnerability management specialists, third-party risk managers, and brand defenders. You will be able to offload more of the high-volume work to your security intelligence solutions by having the software automatically correlate threat data, produce risk scores, identify false positives, and much more.

CAUTION

When you evaluate security intelligence solutions, examine the level to which they employ automation. Is automation confined to aggregating and cross-referencing data, or does the solution add context that equips your teams to make risk-based decisions with confidence? Keep in mind that inputting more raw data into your security intelligence software only adds value if it's automatically analyzed, organized, and delivered to you in an easy-to-consume format.

Integrating security intelligence with processes and infrastructure

Integrating a security intelligence solution into your existing systems is an effective way to make the intelligence accessible and usable without overwhelming teams with new technologies.

A key part of integration involves ensuring that your security intelligence software has visibility into the security events and activities captured by your existing security and network tools. Combining and correlating internal and external data points produces genuine intelligence that is both relevant to your business and placed in the context of the wider threat landscape.

The other critical aspect of integration is delivering the most important, specific, relevant, and contextualized intelligence to the right group at the right time. To accomplish this, integrate your security intelligence solution with your SIEM and other security tools, either through APIs or via interfaces developed in partnership with the security tool vendors.

TIP: When you evaluate security intelligence solutions, it's important to understand which ones easily integrate with your existing software and support your security teams' use cases.

Getting experts to nurture internal experts

The value you get from security intelligence is directly related to your ability to make it relevant to your organization and apply it to existing and new security processes.

You will reach these goals faster if you work with a vendor or consultant that provides technical capabilities and expertise that empower your organization to get the most from security intelligence. As time goes on, working with such a partner will enable members of your team to become security intelligence experts in their own right.

DON'T FORGET: Look for partners that have a wide and deep bench of security intelligence experts. These specialists should have the knowledge and experience to understand your needs in order to assist you in realizing the most value from your investment. Be sure they will be available when you call on their expertise, and that they will work with you to identify new advantages from leveraging security intelligence in your organization. Your chosen partners must be committed to your success today and continue to support your security teams as you move forward.

ON THE WEB: Find more information on selecting the right security intelligence solution by downloading "The Buyer's Guide to Intelligence," from Recorded Future. It includes a handy RFP template to use in evaluating the capabilities of different vendors.

Start Simple and Scale Up

Security intelligence is not a monolith that needs to be dropped onto the security organization all at one time. Instead, you have options in how you collect, process, analyze, and disseminate security intelligence to various stakeholders and groups.

You may choose to start simple with your current staff (instead of building a dedicated security intelligence team), a few data sources, and integration with existing security tools like your SIEM and vulnerability management system. Soon, you may benefit from scaling up with dedicated staff, more data sources, more tools integrations, and more automated workflows, as shown in Figure 14-1.

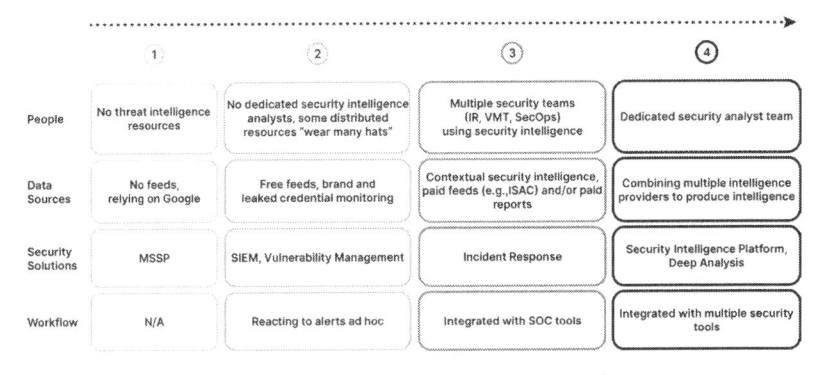

	1	2	3	4
People	No threat intelligence resources	No dedicated security intelligence analysts, some distributed resources "wear many hats"	Multiple security teams (IR, VMT, SecOps) using security intelligence	Dedicated security analyst team
Data Sources	No feeds, relying on Google	Free feeds, brand and leaked credential monitoring	Contextual security intelligence, paid feeds (e.g., ISAC) and/or paid reports	Combining multiple intelligence providers to produce intelligence
Security Solutions	MSSP	SIEM, Vulnerability Management	Incident Response	Security Intelligence Platform, Deep Analysis
Workflow	N/A	Reacting to alerts ad hoc	Integrated with SOC tools	Integrated with multiple security tools

Figure 14-1: Four stages of security intelligence program maturity — from no internal resources to a fully staffed and highly automated program.

Start your journey by researching the needs of each group in your cybersecurity organization and determining how security intelligence will enable them achieve their objectives.

Over time, you will be able to build toward a comprehensive security intelligence program that:

- ☑ Scours the widest possible range and variety of technical, open, and dark web sources
- ☑ Uses automation to deliver easily consumable intelligence
- ☑ Provides fully contextualized alerts in real time with limited false positives
- ☑ Integrates with and enhances your other security technologies and processes
- ☑ Consistently improves the efficiency and efficacy of your entire security organization

Chapter 15

Developing Your Core Security Intelligence Team

In this chapter

- Understand the processes, people, and technology that make up a dedicated security intelligence capability
- Learn how these teams use security intelligence to judge risk and drive business continuity
- Review ways to engage with security intelligence communities

"Talent wins games, but teamwork and intelligence win championships."

— Michael Jordan

We have seen how security intelligence benefits your security teams. Now here are a few suggestions about how to organize your core team dedicated to security intelligence.

Dedicated, but Not Necessarily Separate

As we discussed in the previous chapter, you may want to start your security intelligence journey with people who continue to play other roles on different security teams in the organization, as well.

Eventually, two questions will likely arise:

1. Should there be a dedicated security intelligence team?
2. Should it be independent, or live inside an existing security group?

The answers are: Yes, and it depends.

A dedicated team is best

As you develop a comprehensive security intelligence program, you will need to build a team that's dedicated to collecting and analyzing threat data and turning it into intelligence. The sole focus of this team will be to provide relevant and actionable intelligence to key stakeholders, including senior executives and members of the board.

Dedication and a broad perspective are required to ensure your team members devote enough time to collecting, processing, analyzing, and disseminating intelligence that provides the greatest value to the organization as a whole. It's critical to avoid the temptation to focus on the intelligence needs of a single group over any other.

Where the team sits depends on your organization

Having a security intelligence team with organizational independence (as shown in Figure 15-1) has its advantages — such as greater autonomy and prestige.

Chapter 15: Developing Your Core Security Intelligence Team | 137

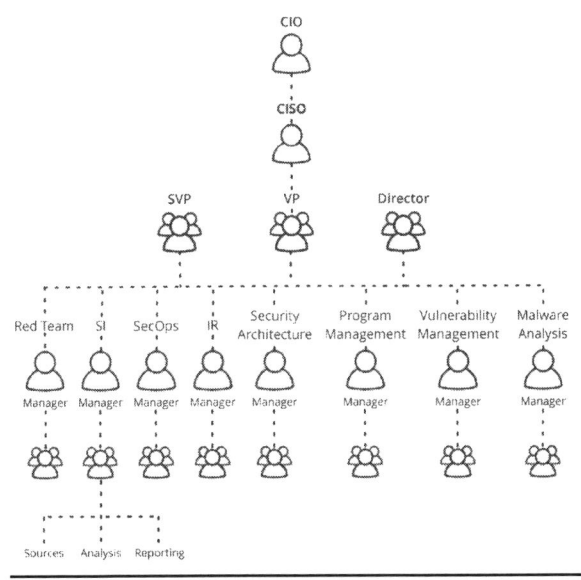

Figure 15-1: Security intelligence as an independent group in the security organizational structure.

However, these advantages may be completely offset by political issues associated with creating a team with a new high-level manager and its own budget that pulls skilled analysts out of their existing groups.

A dedicated security intelligence team does not necessarily need to be a separate function reporting directly to a VP or the CISO. It may instead belong to a group that already works with security intelligence. In many cases this will be the incident response team. Taking this approach is often a viable option to avoid conflict with entrenched security teams.

Picking the People

If you take a gradual approach to building your core security intelligence team, start with individuals who are already in the security organization and are currently applying security intelligence to their particular areas of expertise. They may not have the title "security intelligence analyst" or see themselves that way at first, but they are likely the most capable people available to form the backbone of your emerging security intelligence group.

Core Competencies

The security intelligence function exists to strengthen every other security team — empowering everyone to better protect the entire organization. It is critical that the security intelligence team includes people who understand the core business, operational workflows, network infrastructure, risk profiles, and the supply chain, as well as the organization's technical infrastructure and software applications.

As the security intelligence team matures, you'll want to add members who are skilled at:

- ☑ Correlating external data with internal telemetry
- ☑ Reverse engineering malware and reconstructing attacks (forensics)
- ☑ Providing threat situational awareness and recommendations for security controls
- ☑ Proactively hunting internal threats, including insider threats
- ☑ Educating employees and customers about cyber threats
- ☑ Engaging with the wider security intelligence community
- ☑ Identifying and managing information sources

You may also want to add staff with diverse backgrounds, including experience outside of information technology. In particular:

- ☑ **Analysts with military and intelligence backgrounds** generally understand how to structure processes for data collection, analysis, and reporting, how to adjust for biases in sources, and how to present intelligence and conclusions in ways that are clear, concise, and tailored for their audience.
- ☑ **Staff members with law enforcement experience** have knowledge about criminal tactics and methods, and are effective at distinguishing fact from opinion.

Collecting and Enriching Threat Data

We discussed data sources data in chapter 2. Here we explore how to work with a range of sources to ensure accuracy and relevance.

The human edge

Security intelligence vendors often provide some types of strategic intelligence, but you may also develop in-house capabilities to gather information about the topics and events that are most relevant to your organization.

For example, you may decide to develop an internal web crawler that analyzes the web page code of the top 5,000 web destinations visited by your employees. This analysis might provide insights into the potential for drive-by download attacks. You could share the insights with the security architecture team to assist them in proposing controls that defend against those attacks. This kind of security intelligence generates concrete data, which is much more useful than anecdotes, conjecture, and generic statistics about attacks.

Additional sources

Proprietary sources that may strengthen your security intelligence resources include:

- ☑ Vendor or ISAC feeds
- ☑ Allow lists
- ☑ Deny lists
- ☑ Security intelligence team research

Combining sources

An automated security intelligence solution enables the security intelligence team to centralize, combine, and enrich data from multiple sources — before the data is ingested by other security systems or viewed by human analysts on security operations teams.

Figure 15-2 shows the elements of such an automated threat solution. In this process, information from a security intelligence vendor is filtered to find data that is important to the organization and specific security teams. Then it is enriched by data from internal security intelligence sources and output in formats that are appropriate for tools including the SIEM, ticketing system, and more. This automated translation of raw data into relevant insights is the essence of security intelligence.

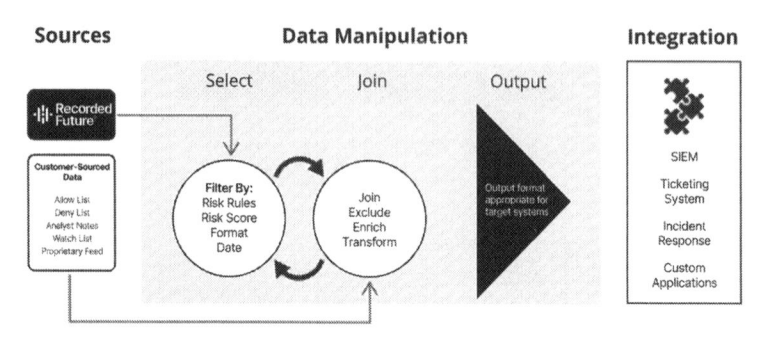

Sources — Recorded Future; Customer-Sourced Data (Allow List, Deny List, Analyst Notes, Watch List, Proprietary Feed)

Data Manipulation — Select (Filter By: Risk Rules, Risk Score, Format, Date); Join (Join, Exclude, Enrich, Transform); Output (Output format appropriate for target systems)

Integration — SIEM, Ticketing System, Incident Response, Custom Applications

Figure 15-2: A security intelligence platform centralizes, combines, and enriches data, and then formats it for multiple target systems. (Source: Recorded Future)

The role of intelligent machines

We've reached the point where automated components have successfully learned the language of threats and are able to accurately identify malicious terms.

Advances in analytics and natural language processing (NLP) bring additional advantages to the security intelligence team. With the right technology, references to threats from all sources are able to be rendered language neutral. This enables humans and machines to analyze them, regardless of the original language the references appeared in.

The combination of analytics and NLP offers huge opportunities for organizations to leverage security intelligence. Not only do these technologies remove language barriers, but they also have the potential to reduce analyst workloads by taking on many tasks related to data collection and correlation.

When combined with the power to consider multiple data and information sources concurrently to produce genuine security intelligence, these capabilities make it far easier to build a comprehensible map of the threat landscape.

Engaging With Security Intelligence Communities

Security intelligence cannot flourish in a vacuum. External relationships are essential to successful security intelligence teams. No matter how advanced your team might be, no single group is as smart as the security intelligence world as a whole.

Many security intelligence communities allow individual organizations to share relevant and timely attack data, enabling other members to protect their organizations before they are victimized. Engaging with trusted communities such as ISACs is crucial for decreasing risk — not just for your individual organization, but also for the entire industry and the cyber world at large. Participation requires time and resources, such as communication with peers via email and attendance at security conferences. However, relationship building must be a priority for security intelligence to be successful.

Conclusion

Using Elite Intelligence to Disrupt Adversaries

"No prudent antagonist thinks light of his adversaries."
— Johann von Goethe

Key Takeaways From the Book

This book began with the idea that intelligence is valuable to everyone across all security functions, and beyond. Intelligence enables teams to anticipate threats, respond to attacks faster, and make better decisions to reduce risk. Throughout this book, we examined how to adopt a proactive, comprehensive approach to security by applying intelligence to several facets of your organization's security strategy.

That's what security intelligence is — an approach that amplifies the effectiveness of security teams and tools by exposing unknown threats, informing better decisions, and driving a shared understanding to accelerate risk reduction across the organization. The six pillars of SecOps intelligence, vulnerability intelligence, threat intelligence, third-party intelligence, brand intelligence, and geopolitical intelligence provide organizations with powerful insight into the risks they face, while streamlining the ways their teams work.

Let's return to the four principles of security intelligence described in the foreword. What results will you achieve when you adopt these principles?

1. You will disrupt the adversaries targeting your organization.

By identifying the adversaries that are most dangerous to your organization and understanding how they work, you will put the right defenses in place and make attackers' lives so difficult that they give up on their efforts to target you.

2. You will gain the context required to make informed decisions and take action.

By generating contextual intelligence that is timely, clear, and actionable, you will enrich your knowledge, simplify decision-making processes, and amplify the impact of all of your security solutions.

3. Your people and machines will work together to increase overall effectiveness.

Machines process and categorize raw data at extraordinary speed and scale, affording humans the time and context they need to perform intuitive, big-picture analysis. By improving human and automated workflows, security intelligence will save time and money, reduce human burnout, and improve security overall.

4. Your security teams — and many others in your organization — will work smarter.

Every security team, as well as executives and colleagues across your organization — from risk management and fraud prevention to brand management and third-party risk, and beyond — will receive more relevant intelligence and less irrelevant raw data. They will be able to interact with the right intelligence at the right time, in formats that are easy to understand, through existing security and collaboration tools. They will be empowered to make better decisions, faster.

One of the great advantages of security intelligence is that it enables you to scale up your program in stages. Start by improving the effectiveness of core activities in security operations, incident response, vulnerability management, and threat intelligence — or by building new foundations for increasingly important programs relating to third-party risk, brand protection, and geopolitical security. Either way, you will achieve measurable wins for your organization at each step. We hope this handbook has provided you with a view of security intelligence's vast potential and how to achieve it.